ABSOLUTELY VULNERABLE

The Crisis of Strategic Business Planning in America

by

THOMAS ALLEN MALM

BRAINWORKS BOOKS
Philadelphia, Pennsylvania

BRAINWORKS BOOKS
The imprint of T.A. Malm & Associates

ISBN: 978-0-578-01686-3

Thomas Allen Malm is available for private consulting, business seminars, strategic planning retreats, and public speaking engagements. Write info@tamalm.com for more information

This book is available with quantity discounts for the use in education and training programs, special promotions, and sales premiums. Contact books@tamalm.com for information.

Attention Booksellers – contact books@tamalm.com for information regarding stocking this book and to schedule an in-store appearance by its author.

T.A. Malm & Associates
Philadelphia, Pennsylvania
www.tamalm.com

For Chris

ABSOLUTELY VULNERABLE

"A warrior's not about perfection, or victory, or invulnerability. He's about absolute vulnerability."

From the movie *Peaceful Warrior*

ABSOLUTELY VULNERABLE
The Crisis of Strategic Business Planning in America

Acknowledgments

Hiromi Gunji deserves my deepest gratitude for his inspiration, mentoring, and support.

I must thank my mother for giving me her exceptional gift for reasoning.

Without my father, this book would never have been written. Frankly, if he were alive today the book would be better.

GETTING TO THE TRUTH

On a red-eye flight from Oakland to Newark I sat in a First Class recliner unable to ignore the encroachment of my aisle-mate. I tried to nap, but the man next to me was deeply engrossed in work. With the flight attendants serving snacks and cocktails, passing out headphones, fluffing pillows and distributing blankets, he remained unrelentingly focused. His computer keys tapped in quick spurts. There seemed to be urgency in each keystroke as his calculator tape curled under the seat. He was flipping through binders, books, briefs, and magazines. It was clear to me that his light was going to burn all night long. Unable to catch any sleep, I became curious to know what he was doing.

With his tie loosened and his white shirt sleeves rolled up, the middle-aged man explained that his job was to find the ideal spot to relocate his company's headquarters. He was filtering through demographic reports, quality-of-life considerations, tax codes, education statistics, municipal incentives, available workforce data, transportation and shipping conveniences, and a range of other factors. "Sounds like a tough job," I commented. The reply was amusing.

"Not at all," he said. "I only need to know where the CEO wants to live and then justify it."

This very true story amplifies the flawed manner in which business in America is often managed. It gives a peek into the fairly common attitude that uses research to justify actions, instead using it to find the kind of information that can safely dictate actions. When you start with the answer, the job becomes easier (imagine if he had to sift through every possible location). Unfortunately, starting with the answer that sets an action in motion also puts you at the risk of missing critical information and potentially threatening consequences.

My aisle-mate's attitude is not unusual, and certainly not hard to understand. Workers always see the benefit in making the boss happy. It's good for one's career to please the head honcho, and in this case, the incentive for the middle manager was to do no more than find enough data to ensure the CEO got to live where he wanted to live. There was no sense that the business he served was vulnerable in any way.

In the work of my aisle-mate, there could have been a grave disconnection between the CEO's wants and the company's needs. The task, as he described it, was designed without focusing on the best case for the business' health and well-being. It was out-of-sync with the basic objective of every enterprise - a company only exists to promote its own health.

This book is about fundamental strategic marketing and the culture of American business. It will discuss why every decision a company makes should be in accord with a market-driven strategy – focused outward to cultivate sustaining revenue from the marketplace for the company's survival. The most successful and enduring businesses in the world work from a formal planning process that limits their exposure to threats. A well-designed strategic plan will contain the best scenarios to ensure the ultimate success of any business.

Strategic planning isn't a process that is used to confirm that you are right. It is a process that realigns your actions with verifiable opportunity and reveals their probable consequences. It becomes a company's road map that shows the smoothest route over the rough terrain of the marketplace. It identifies where you are weak and threatened. It verifies the facts against which you make your decisions and guide your enterprise. It's the keystone of any meaningful chance that a company will endure.

If you are looking for a book that will tell you the twelve steps to driving more customers to your business by the end of the week, it's probably somewhere else on the shelf. This one isn't it. That book would be about true marketing in the same way a life preserver is about swimming. Real marketing isn't about immediate gratification, magical gimmicks and schemes, or quick fixes. Real marketing creates clear vision, obtainable objectives, and long-term stability.

Instead of providing instant solutions, this book promises the kind of help that makes your company healthier, competitors less competitive, and customers more prevalent. It discusses the science, craft, and art of strategic market planning and its execution with anecdotes and examples that hopefully will be useful in your thinking and planning for your business. It isn't in the form of most "self-help" books in which even the dimmest dolt could benefit. It offers simple principles to be used in complex environments to test, track, evaluate and act. This is a book for smart people.

The following pages are rife with examples where the fundamental principles of marketing were followed to the letter and the result, regardless of the condition of the market, was growth and success. You will also see generous examples of failure, in good economic times and bad, where some aspect of the fundamental marketing principles were not adhered to, or even ignored. There are many examples to illustrate why structured and proven strategic planning is the only path to a business' most assured successes.

Marketing's definition is to deliver goods and services to customers systematically and profitably. The operative word is "systematic." Marketing by its definition, means following a system that ensures you have solutions to address the needs of specifically targeted customers in such a way that appeals to them, *regardless of whatever else is taking place in the market*. The system must include specific goals, be applicable in the current conditions to maximize the potential of the enterprise, and it must be in accord with the enterprise's long-term objectives. Simple as it sounds, that is the only way a company can sustain itself for any period of time.

Unfortunately, pure marketing is rarely executed. It takes time that experienced people who are comfortable with their success find pointless. The most significant influences that kill a strategic planning process (and the successful adherence to basic marketing principles) are human factors. Real marketing takes courage. It demands intelligence. It begins by being able to take a look at your company for what it really is, assessing your opportunities honestly against any factor that may influence your situation, and strategically organizing yourself in a manner that advances your position.

There are those who believe they have some advantage because of their long years of experience. As a result, any change in the conditions of the market that are not anticipated and planned for, and that do not fall within the knowledge gained through this experience, creates an opportunity for the company to fail. In a dynamic world, this is like carrying the company, its customers that have grown to depend on it, and all of its employees, for a walk on a circus high wire. You might endure, but maybe not without losing something along the way. You just might crash.

What makes the practice of strategic marketing so perfect for all businesses is that it is "industry neutral." It is a process that lets us test what we know against the dynamics of the market. It recognizes that experience is a factor but not always an advantage. The influence of experience, education, training, basic IQ, corporate politics, quality of competition, home life, individual upbringing, personal financial needs, and work habits can be as damaging to a company as they can be to its success. To understand how these influences can be organized to benefit an enterprise requires the ability to step back and look objectively. That's what a formal planning process can bring to a company. Through disciplined market planning principles, all elements of a business are evaluated and restructured if needed to give the company its best advantage in spite of its biases, weaknesses, or current position.

When major brands and companies in America struggle and fail, it is not always the result of some outside, uncontrollable influence. Some are just poorly run from plans that are faulty. Many have no plan at all beyond the original entrepreneur's vision. Some fail only because of the chief executive's experience and comfort level. Sure, maybe there are demographic shifts, the culture evolves, the economy tightens, or a natural disaster steps in to influence a market. But, the extent to which these changing conditions affect a company's business is directly related to the company's attention to business planning.

The correct mindset for strategic planning is to acknowledge absolute vulnerability. Once that acknowledgment is lost, the urgency goes away. The competitive drive disappears. The defensive posture is relaxed. Hubris emerges and the decision makers forget that every decision has a consequence that could end up being fatal to the business. Depending on their strength and perceived invulnerability, decisions might be based on unchallenged assumptions, irrelevant or obsolete experience, or an incomplete observation. Regardless of your business, there are threats from within the organization and from the outside environment that can consume you. Taking the time to research, study, evaluate, and learn about all of the elements of your company and the marketplace in which it does business, reduces surprises and can minimize their effect.

A strategic plan doesn't just reduce the possibility of a company failing. Companies that fail to plan are often missing opportunities by not being aware of market changes, useful applications of new technology, or a competitor's weaknesses. Smaller companies may see a more formidable competitor as insurmountable. But if you know where to target, you can reduce the most imposing competitive threat. Changes in the marketplace can produce new opportunities. Demographic evolutions, community growth, new distribution channels, the demise of a competitor, and newly discovered technologies can shuffle the order of a marketplace. Relying on the principles of formal strategic planning will add focus that detects and confirms opportunities. To not plan is irresponsible.

IF THERE'S A WILL

It's probably a good idea to begin with an example of how the formal strategic planning process can transform a company. It is an example of exceptional success derived from the right combination of formal planning, corporate culture, and leadership. It's a story of prosperity divined from the seemingly dismal prospects of one company's core businesses that shows, how against the odds, a company can be led to reinvention and survival. With a realistic plan focused on specific objectives, sometimes the results are absolutely remarkable.

The Japanese company that has done business between the American shores longer than any other is Brother International. I joined them from the mid-1980's to the early 1990's. From 1954, until just before I came on board, Brother's US Business grew to $200 million in revenue. Their sales-driven strategy earned a strong position in the consumer typewriter, office equipment, and sewing machine markets behind strong American brands like IBM, Smith-Corona, and Singer. They were also an established presence in the commercial sewing machine business that served the American textile market. The company was successful, growing, and prosperous. But it was also threatened.

During the 1980's, consumer-level typewriters were on the verge of becoming irrelevant. The entry-level sewing machine products held a secondary position against a dominant brand, in a market that would reach a saturation point as the consumers in the Baby Boom generation made their once-in-a-lifetime purchase. The US textile industry that purchased commercial equipment from Brother International was chasing cheap labor off our shores to Asia and across the border to

Mexico. Add to these dismal conditions the fact that the currency exchange rate between the US dollar and the Yen, which afforded the company its aggressive price position for so many years, was becoming dramatically more challenging. Just a few years before these conditions began to evolve into potential trouble, a Japanese CEO, Hiromi Gunji, took over the American division of Brother.

When Gunji arrived in America to run the company, he announced that his goal was to achieve $1 billion in annual revenue within ten years. Considering the $200 million dollar starting point and the conditions of the time, we all thought there must be something in his tea. But he was confident in the strategic market planning processes he introduced, the management-by-objective incentives initiated, and the work culture he fostered. It was a radical change, and not every person in the organization adapted. He reorganized the company's divisions, and in some cases, installed new leadership. There were tough decisions made. In the end, he achieved his lofty billion-dollar ambition a year ahead of plan.

The most important aspect of the company culture under Gunji may have been his market-focused strategic planning/product management philosophy, and its promotion of fresh perspectives and ideas. He encouraged shaking up the status quo. He never wanted anyone to feel too comfortable. But he wanted everyone with a thoughtful opinion, regardless of how much it may conflict with the conventional ideas guiding the company, to feel free expressing it. He abhorred recklessness. He respected a well-prepared and fact-based disagreement. It was a culture where brilliance flourished.

Flourishing brilliance is rare in many corporate environments, and it is only occasionally found beyond the founding entrepreneurs in most small businesses. The IQ of an individual can have a huge impact on the organization if that individual is schooled, trained, and prepared to employ his or her brilliance to the strategic goals of the company. Yet, that individual's intelligence can be dulled by the collective IQ of the company through its structure and culture. It isn't uncommon for bosses to hire and promote personnel with whom they are comfortable. Occasionally, that can mean they simply surround themselves with people that they can count on to never challenge their brilliance, and as such, they may not be hiring to improve the company. The environment at Gunji's Brother was dynamic and demanding, the mission was always clear, and everyone was challenged to be their best.

Brother had an "open door" policy that encouraged any employee to visit any executive if they had an issue or problem to resolve. It was a policy established by the company's original founders in Japan. I once took advantage of it for a private meeting with the CEO. I expressed some concern about how my Divisional Vice President might respond. Gunji replied by stating that any leader in the company that would feel threatened by our private meeting is too weak to be a leader in the company (consequently, my direct boss had no quarrel with this). An Executive Vice President serving with Gunji once told me that I could feel comfortable enough to argue with him "up to the point where I get fired." Although the statement had a Zen-like quality, it ensured an open and free expression of ideas as long as they were respectful. To encourage the conviction of one's ideas, even when they opposed his own, was a manner of extruding truth and ensuring progress of the company.

One component that was part of ensuring that the opinions of staff members could be trusted was the company's open sharing of information to all those who make decisions. P&L statements, sales and inventory plans, customer records and other vital information were not strictly and securely held between only a limited few – they became an openly shared report card for anyone with a stake in the company's accomplishments as they were gauged against the goals of the strategic plan.

When I worked for Gunji and Company, I got the sense that there was no assumption that shouldn't be questioned. There was no information that shouldn't be challenged. He established a culture that was doggedly determined not to get it wrong. I was amused when a young

Japanese co-worker told me that his wife had taken a home pregnancy test. "It read positive," he said. Then he added, "I took it, too . . . It was negative."

Confirming information and "testing the test" in this manner was the kind of habit one picks up from not trusting things on their face value. It's a habit that you develop after acknowledging that there can be things that threaten you that you might not be able to imagine.

A generation of business people who grew up in Japan when Gunji did could understand the profound cost of a reckless reliance on untested information. The Potsdam Declaration, which outlined the terms for Japan's surrender during World War II, promised "the inevitable and complete destruction of the Japanese armed forces and just as inevitably the utter devastation of the Japanese homeland." It was probably unimaginable to them, based on the constant bombing they were receiving, that the Allied promise was both precisely accurate and absolutely deliverable. From their experience they "knew" the capabilities of the Allies and were unmoved by the promise of devastation. They refused to accept the terms of the declaration. As a result, two cities and all of their citizens were annihilated by use of atomic weapons. They never wanted to be so arrogant to suffer again from such a misjudgment.

Behind the strategic planning process installed by Brother International's new leader was a realization that any new development in the marketplace, whether it has or hasn't made it onto your radar, can be a threat to the business. Your survival and absolute vulnerability is a pressing reason to know exactly what threats the changing market conditions can bring. A new technology, an upstart competitor, a changing fashion or fad, a demographic evolution, and an economic shift all can all come with issues that need addressing.

Few people who work in a company with a well-established brand ever think anything bad will happen to them until it is too late. Just as the military minds advising the Emperor of Japan believed that they understood the capabilities of the US, many companies suffer because they fail to imagine their vulnerability. They don't accept threats as realistic.

A good example of the environment that Gunji set can be described by the company's growth to leadership in the facsimile business. In the mid-1980's, the product category was barely established in the consumer business channel, but the demand was exploding. Facsimile products were not a new idea - major corporations were using them for years. But faxing had typically been expensive and slow. In the 1980's, technology and price made them more practical to use and financially accessible to a critical mass of small business consumers.

The initial product that Brother introduced in the new era of faxing was an engineering marvel. It was a two-color thermal paper machine, transmitting and receiving in red and black. Nearly every key competitor in the office products business had a fax machine, but none of them had such a feature. It was a bona fide marketing first. Unfortunately, Brother misjudged the value of this benefit to the consumer.

The key benefit of a fax machine in the late 1980's was the product's ability to communicate efficiently, and to reduce the cost of the long distance phone bill. The market leaders were sending a typical page in well under a minute. Brother's two-color machine couldn't meet the expectation. The cost of transmitting a long distance fax on a Brother machine could cost up to twice as much as the accepted standard. The technological breakthrough of two-color faxing inherently hampered the ability to address the primary consumer need - speed.

Brother's innovative machine was also impractical. The two-color faxing technology didn't work unless the person you were faxing had the same model. In practice, anyone with a two-color Brother Fax machine would most likely be sending documents to someone who owned a faster black-only model from the competitors. Two-color faxing was technically unique but it failed to connect with the consumer's needs and wants. Speed and functionality were the primary selling points.

With a marketplace flooded with product choices, the last factor for success was the sharpness of a product's pricing. The competition was intense. In the order of the business at the time, stronger brand names like Canon, Sharp, and Panasonic hit the market with aggressive pricing and meaningful features. A fast and functional Murata-branded machine defined the category's expectation for minimum performance and value with a street price of $995. The two-color Brother machines accrued dust in the warehouse because of their slow speed and retail selling price of over $1,500. This version of "the cutting-edge" wasn't anything anyone was buying.

With this initial misstep, Brother went back to the drawing board a bit wiser and much more determined. The next generation of Brother facsimile machines was developed by focusing on the lessons they learned. They acquired a keen understanding of the key factors for success. But there was still a risk. Considering the rapid advance of technology and the intense battleground for shelf space, it was hard to imagine the innovations and values that would be built into the next generation of machines from the bigger and more established competing manufacturers. The product development group in Japan got aggressive and came through with what was believed would be an attention-getting value-proposition for the consumer. It had more features and more speed than anything anyone had seen yet. But there was no telling what the others in the competition would introduce.

Based on these slick new machines developed in Japan, the Product Development/Product Management Department at Brother in the United States introduced a goal to gain a 5% share of the market. It was thought to be a cautious and soundly attainable projection, even though it meant the company's growth plan was to improve by at least 1000%. The goal was based on the stronger established market position of the competition, and a reasonable expectation for market acceptance based on the new generation of product's features and value. But it was also based on the accepted traditions of the distribution channel.

A much different goal was presented by the sales division. According to their strategic planning process, the marketplace was seeing dramatic shifts in how products would be distributed to consumers. The paradigm that had shaped opportunity in the channel for the previous two decades was being replaced. Understanding that there was a new and evolving set of key success factors, the sales division presented an argument demonstrating a need for a the goal to be at least 15% of the market or Brother was "out of the fax business." Their case revealed a narrow potential for success that was impossible to ignore.

The retail channels were changing dramatically. Catalog showrooms like Service Merchandise were disappearing. The department store channel, characterized by Macy's and others, was taking away retail floor space in the hard goods departments. Mass merchandisers like Wal-Mart were tightening up their product plans to ensure the best revenue production from their shelf space. New retailers were emerging, bringing a new business model for successful marketing of office products to consumers and small businesses.

In the previous paradigm, the department stores and catalog showrooms would select as many products from all the respected brands as their merchandising space would allow. The office machine merchandise plan would generally carry the key products from Brother, Smith-Corona, Panasonic, Sharp, and Canon. Each manufacturer might display five or six models from each product category – typewriters, copiers, fax machines, calculators, etc. The manufacturers would put together a program that included generous financial support to the retailer for display space, dedicated catalog pages, frequent inclusion in flyers and advertising, additional market development funds, mark down dollars, and liberal unsold product return policies. In practice, the consumer-recognized brands would buy their retail space and fund their own success. The consumer in this scenario would be given a wide breadth of choices and the success of any brand depended on winning a head-to-head battle on the showroom floor of the store. It's the way business was done in the home office product category for decades. This was all changing.

The massive Baby Boom generation grew into homeowners. To serve this customer profile, the catalog showroom and department store's hard goods categories were supplanted by the category specific "power retailers" and specialty retail chains. Home Depot and Lowe's were the places to shop for one's home maintenance and improvement projects. Best Buy and Circuit City were becoming the source for electronics and home entertainment products. Specialty stores like Staples, Office Max, Office Depot and the membership warehouse clubs like Costco and Sam's were the place to buy supplies and machines for the small business and home office.

These emerging channels brought a different approach for merchandising goods to the consumer. Product selections were narrow. The value of the merchant's shelf space was measured in product turnover instead of the amount of merchandising dollars a manufacturer was willing to give the retailer. In effect, success no longer was tied to positioning yourself to win a consumer battle on the retailer's showroom floor. The retailer's merchandise buyer selected the best consumer values at each price point to fit defined revenue production needs for every square inch of shelf space. The store's merchandise buyer narrowed the consumer's decisions by exposing them to just the products deemed to be the best.

The impact of this new business model had a profound effect on the projected opportunity for a manufacturer. Success in the evolving retail marketplace began by winning the buyer's favor. There wasn't room in the retailer's merchandising plan to give shelf space to every formidable brand, regardless of their strong consumer recognition. There might be fewer than three suppliers selected for the product category. According to the new rules for achievement in this new retailing scenario, if you couldn't be important enough to the store's merchandise buyer to represent 15% of the revenue in the category, the consumer would never see your brand.

This perspective was presented by Brother's sales division. The analysis of information recognized the vulnerability of the situation. There was not a wide range of success available. Gunji had always said that the "end-user is King," yet in our business model it was important to remember that the retail merchandise buyer was "Queen." In the changing paradigm of the business, his philosophy became eminently important. There was no way we could ever get to serve the King unless we made the Queen very happy.

The product development group responded. The scenario didn't just influence top-side revenue. There was a supply side impact, too. The difference between 5% and 15% changed manufacturing economies. This greater marketshare requirement allowed an aggressive rethinking of the whole feature-value quotient and the development of an extraordinary product line to serve any King. The Queen was pleased.

Because of their culture, Brother was prepared and quickly adapted to the opportunity, dictated new standards for the category, and grabbed the leadership position. It was a result of not just noticing that there were some new retailers to sell, but from correctly assessing their impact on the bigger picture to realize what their proliferation would mean to consumer traffic, the selling paradigm, and the real opportunity for those competing for shelf space. That was only revealed through the process that required the company to step back, reevaluate the conditions of the market, and position itself to lead.

THE INSOLUBLE PROBLEM

"We are continually faced by great opportunities brilliantly disguised as insoluble problems." That's what Lee Iacocca said when he was selected as the one to save Chrysler in the 1980's. He had previously been the President of Ford Motor Company where he unsuccessfully pushed original ideas (like the concept for the "K" Car and the minivan that he took with him to Chrysler) and offered strong opinions about how the company needed to compete. He had a powerful personality and in no way could be described as a "Yes Man." He was an innovator, and CEO Henry Ford II must not have wanted these qualities in the leader of his company. He was fired in spite of posting a $2 billion profit.

On the day Iacocca was hired by Chrysler, the company was the least significant of the Big Three and the most vulnerable to the market pressures that had been mounting for over a decade. Toyota and Datsun nameplates were appearing on the cars in American driveways. The consumer appeal of these emerging brands eroded the market position of all US manufacturers. To make things worse, Chrysler-made Dodge Aspens and Plymouth Volares had been hit by serious recall issues that damaged consumer confidence in Chrysler products. The insoluble problems Iacocca spoke of were born from a combination of financial, quality, image, and competitive realities. Without major changes, the terrible state of his struggling company left him with little chance against the challenges in the new order of the competitive American automobile market.

All three of the major American automobile manufacturers had been caught off-guard by the needs and wants of an evolving US consumer through the 1970's. The core customer-base, composed of WWII-era consumers, was being replaced by their children. The Big Three manufacturers hadn't anticipated what this would mean. They hadn't imagined that the Baby Boomers would be a new kind of consumer that wanted something other than what they were selling. They hadn't planned for it. The Japanese manufacturers had.

In terms of timing, it would have been pointless for the Japanese manufacturers to have launched in America any sooner. They clearly must have understood the conditions of the marketplace in America from 1940 through the 1960's, and patiently accepted that there wasn't much probability of selling cars to the generation that came-of-age during World War II. Those consumers had Pearl Harbor embedded in their psyche as a defining moment of their lives. In an effort to fortify support for the defeat of Japan during World War II, this American generation had been influenced by Defense Department propaganda and news reels that characterized the Japanese as a "yellow hoard" of crazed kamikazes. Negative attitudes toward the Japanese were found deep in the core of the US consumers in the '50's and 60's. Yet, in the 1970's, this World War II generation's children were to become the largest consumer force in history. They had no connection to the kind of emotions that were stirring in the hearts of their parents.

Seeing a new and emerging consumer base, the Japanese automobile manufacturers took a disciplined and strategic approach to the US marketplace. They studied the culture, learned the habits, and understood the desires of a new consumer power. They saw exploitable gaps that were being unmet by the product offerings from Detroit. They didn't operate from past experience or intuitive hunches. They confirmed their information. They waited patiently for the conditions to evolve to give them an advantage.

In the 1960's, Detroit swaggered into the market, and stirred consumer imaginations with "Pony Cars." They bolted obscene levels of horsepower into cars with badges that said SS, GTO, 442, RS, and GTX. Chargers, Challengers and Mustangs were rockets with a measure of appeal that was reduced to elapsed times clocked in quarter-mile distances. They showed cylinder displacement numbers on their fenders, from 289 to 496 cubic inches. In the view of Detroit during the 1960's, "huge" was good. Status came from metal monuments with massive horsepower. It was all about wearing as much iron and chrome as possible while beating the guy in the other car to the next stop light. Six-miles-to-a-gallon of gas was hardly a consideration. By 1970, Japan positioned cars boasting economy and reliability strongly in the minds of the consumer, just before Detroit started seeing the first gas shortages and high insurance rates for American performance cars. Detroit was not prepared.

Japanese manufacturers were looking ahead of the consumer wants of the day. They were adopting technologies and best practices from around the world to address the wants and needs that the next generation of consumers would have. The market would see a predictable shift in the control of fossil fuel. The insurance industry lobbied to curtail the muscle cars that tempted unsafe operation. The Japanese manufacturers answered the new consumer's concerns regarding the environment. With sleeker designs and improved performance they penetrated the US with a segmented long-term strategy.

Toyota initially partnered with the strongest established dealers possible. They found their market in the niche created by the changing conditions of the day. They operated underneath the arrogance of Detroit's position of leadership. Eventually, as fuel prices doubled, the Toyota and Datsun brands became a topic for consumers at the office water cooler. "I just drove up to Buffalo and back. Only cost me $3.00 in gas."

The product spoke to the needs of a new car consumer. Toyota capsulated their message and targeted the masses of drivers looking for reliable economy and performance. They drove a hard public relations campaign, enlisting the endorsements of every important consumer publication and automobile reviewer. They worked with the top agencies in America to develop effective ad campaigns. They understood the people, the place, and the price threshold, and promoted their goods with expected results.

As demand grew for Toyota automobiles, they used the muscle of their popular consumer success to require dealers make their franchises exclusively Toyota. Toyota created a consumer pull for their unique automobiles that gave them market power. It would take years of ground-up engineering and expensive retooling from every Detroit manufacturer and supplier to match the Japanese models in a head-to-head feature battle. The Big Three were in the unimaginable position of reacting to this threat. Products like the Chevy Chevette were not a matching value-proposition. The Ford Pinto (a product from the Iacocca period) was not a viable competitive answer. Chrysler turned to Mitsubishi to import Japanese cars with their American nameplate. At each point in the marketing mix, the strategic thinkers from Japan executed a comprehensive and detailed plan for gaining consumer trust and cultivating new buying habits with them.

When bringing automobiles to the US market, the Japanese capitalized on several vulnerabilities of the Detroit manufacturing giants. American cars had limited life-spans and were not durable beyond 50,000 miles. It was "planned obsolescence" encouraged by the same belief that suggests that the invention of the light bulb was not genius – the genius was the invention of the light bulb that burned out. The market was a closed competition between three forces with long histories and established predictability. The three main manufacturers built cars by the same standards and aspired for no great achievements in endurance. Whether or not Detroit had the technology to build cars that could last for 150,000 miles was irrelevant. There was no motivation to take it to market. Better-built goods in the pre-1970's business model were bad for business.

American cars consumed an inefficient volume of gasoline. They were polluters. The US manufacturers were challenged by new Environmental Protection Agency standards for fuel economy and rules that required all manufacturers to post gas mileage performance numbers on the windows of their cars. They had no choice but to react with investments to retool, reengineer, and remarket themselves. That would take time, so they also reacted with lobbying and legal actions to delay or reduce any imposing requirements. They couldn't respond with any agility. Higher gas prices would send shoppers looking for alternatives. Many customers were lost.

The Japanese entered the US market with the advantage of the cheap yen, lower labor costs, and market-friendly products. The Japanese strategy was to systematically capture market and beat the US manufacturers in a race to meet a newly defined consumer and its demand for automobiles. They knew that the emerging consumer's wants would fit a new standard, shaped by economic and ecological factors.

In the 1980's, there was an opportunity within this insoluble problem and Lee Iacocca was among the few in the American automobile industry to see it. He was the right guy, at the right time, to restore confidence in Chrysler. He had melded his fundraising skills, engineering acumen, and salesmanship into an irresistible offer that appealed to our needs and wants on a range of levels. Iacocca brought the magic and imagination that was needed to make the case that would be appealing to the American people, not just in the retail showrooms, but also as the prospective lenders who would help him save the Chrysler brand. He set the stage for the company to borrow from the Federal and various State governments so they could completely revamp the product line, retool the factories, and address the needs of the American consumer.

The Iacocca led Chrysler introduced newly designed products like the "K-car" and the mini van. He offered purchase incentives like cash rebates with the slogan, "Buy a car, get a check." Quickly, his plan revealed a reason for optimism. Consumers did buy cars and get checks – and like the phoenix, Chrysler rose from its challenges, repaid its loans, and was restored as a formidable force.

Iacocca's most important slogan was not his discount message. At the time when American consumers were not yet completely comfortable buying the products they wanted from a foreign supplier, he challenged them. "If you can find a better car, buy it." He understood the competition and the consumers in the marketplace. He recognized where the company's opportunity was for re-invention and exploited it with products that earned the brand a unique position. He promoted his new products with a message that encouraged the consumer's curiosity and gained its confidence.

Iacocca had a vision for what a US manufacturer could become and a plan to see it to fruition. He knew where the company could compete for market most successfully. He had an understanding of the consumer and most surly operated from a design to help the company survive the new order of the industry. Chrysler made products people wanted, that filled niches that the other US competitors didn't, and promoted them in a manner that motivated consumers to make a buying habit change.

With a second chance and a new product line, Chrysler earned a great deal of media attention. Their promotional campaigns were very effective in telling their new story. The factory rebate was a useful tool that motivated reluctant consumers to kick a few tires and take a test drive. At the time, this pricing tool was in balance with the rest of the marketing mix.

The successes of the US auto industry in the 1950's and 60's were the product of a business environment that for years suggested there was no reason for the major manufacturers in Detroit to fear losing position. The US automobile industry was a huge and gigantic economic force ever since Henry Ford figured out how to deliver cars *en mass*. The Detroit model for the Automobile industry had been mostly based on an idea introduced by GM's Alfred P. Sloan in the 1920's, in which all the plans and solutions were generated from the top. As long as the US boarders weren't threatened by imports targeting the Big Three's rightful customer base, that management style worked.

The leading Detroit-based manufacturers stood in the 1960's as a power with experience and wealth. Their employees made above average wages from plum factory jobs. Their benefits were first class. Yet, the relationship between the labor unions and the car companies was adversarial and out-of-sync with the changing competitiveness of the marketplace. Wages were high and benefits were rich, yet the quality produced was below the standard set by the market invading competitors.

Being blinded by their success, the manufacturers and labor unions in the US auto industry missed what the Japanese industry didn't. Success itself does not ensure sustainable success. Consumers determine what their needs are based on the influences of the world around them. The US automobile industry priced themselves out of the market with obsolete goods. They were so pleased with their performance in a non-competitive environment that they missed the fact that intelligent consumers expected better. The opportunity the Detroit manufacturers delivered to Nissan and Toyota was born from an indifference to the needs of the American consumer. The brain trust within the Big Three manufacturers developed automobiles that did not address the key buying "hot buttons" of a new and formidable generation of consumers. Highly compensated union workers bolted these cars together with no real attention to the fit and finish. Dealers would make the fixes - maybe. The leadership of the major US car manufacturing giants, and their supporting labor unions, never anticipated a generation of consumers that wouldn't defend the shores by "buying American."

Today the "insoluble" problem that the US automaker faces is itself. For over 30 years they had a chance to get better, but never made the strategic organizational changes necessary to address real competitive challenges. The labor unions needed to change in fundamental ways that they refused to recognize. Both are now worse off than any time in their history. They not only opened the door for foreign-made goods, but they also created the opportunity for the foreign-owned companies to beat them on our own soil using American workers producing goods in foreign-owned plants.

How can that be? The debatable answer is that The Big Three and organized labor just aren't very good at planning. They either fail to compete, or have little idea of how to compete effectively. Naturally, when the three leading automakers stood before Congress asking the American people for an injection of cash in 2008, they weren't received with a wave of sympathy.

Like any lender, when I listened to the Congressional hearings, I was listening for hope that America's investment in their vision was not a fool's folly. What was their plan to make me want to buy their cars again? That was my litmus test. What fundamental and strategic actions were they planning that would neutralize the competitive strengths of the foreign producers and position their products with competitive favor in the minds of the majority of the consumers in North America? I was looking for something long-range that anticipated the needs of consumers five years from now. How are they planning to address the next generation of consumers? A glimpse into their imaginations did not translate into restored confidence.

Ford had been intoxicated for a decade by SUV sales when gasoline was cheap. They had to have seen US fuel prices as unstable because of the increased demand in so many highly populated and emerging countries like India and China. But, until the $4 price hit here at home and rendered their product line impotent, they pushed on with astounding confidence. Reacting to the impact high fuel prices had on their gas guzzling trucks, they turned to a plan that will eventually deliver hybrids and a new Ford Fiesta. They intend to use these new cars to address the emerging "green generation's" transportation needs and wants. Yet, because the strategic planning practitioners in Japan have been focusing on this emerging generation of consumers for nearly a decade, Ford has a tough challenge to reclaim marketshare with "green conscious consumers."

Ford's success with a "green" strategy will come if the benefits they offer consumers are significantly more appealing than the benefits delivered by the Japanese brands that have already established leadership in this segment. The plan, and its execution, must be focused. The car and its nameplate must identify with the "green consumer's" purpose. Their promotions must demonstrate a credible contact with the consumer's key concerns for value, performance, economy, and ecological impact. Ford's major ad campaign in early 2009 focused on rugged trucks while Toyota filled their commercials with the ultimate "green" vision, telling the consumer that their company is evolving toward zero-emission automobiles that "create no waste in any way" and result in a neutral impact on the environment. The contrasting campaigns have created a position for each brand in the mind of the consumer.

Meanwhile, GM has invested their future in an electric car they call The Volt. Will this model reset the order of the auto market? Maybe. But its introduction as a state-of-the-art innovation is already behind China's BYD electric cars which started production late in 2008. The Chinese cars are gradually being rolled out to the world's markets with a US campaign planned just in time to create concerns for GM. Whether the BYD car is any good or not remains to be seen over time. Yet, GM must be concerned.

BYD's electric automobile costs a consumer little more than half of the roll-out price for The Volt. Its battery has a range that out-distances the projected performance of The Volt by 50%. Not only is this car expected to have broad consumer appeal, Warren Buffett's company, Berkshire Hathaway, has invested $1.8 billion for 9.9% of BYD. That helps give the Chinese manufacturer universal credibility and market building power.

BYD's position doesn't mean the game is over for GM. It just means the stakes are higher. Because the public relations campaign has built high performance expectations for The Volt, it must not only work as promised, it must be good enough to set the standard for the category and engage the mass support of consumers. It must neutralize any threats from Japan, Germany, Korea, and China. It must take a leading position in consumer automobiles that GM hasn't held for years.

Because they have asked for our confidence (and money), it is fair for Americans to ask the CEO's of GM and Chrysler how they will take marketshare from Toyota, Nissan and Honda. Are there solid and strategically derived action plans that will transform customers for American-branded cars from Toyota hybrid owners? In this economic war for the American automobile industry's survival, will the US taxpayers be funding a revamping of the corporate culture that has allowed the companies to get whipped in the dealer showroom day-in and day-out for the last forty years, or would the handout from the American people simply help them get through the next expense cycle so they can continue failing with a business model that doesn't work. Will the investment be to support a culture that is comfortable with a product evolution that trails the innovation of foreign producers by at least one generation, or will they engage in a war for marketshare that re-establishes America as a world power and the standard bearer for technology and value?

As they stood asking for the American people's faith and trust, the competence of the men running these companies was questioned by Congress. A few US Representatives suggested they step down. On morning television, GM's Rick Wagoner explained that dealing with the current crisis required the most talented people possible. He said his team at GM is "experienced, knows the business, and knows the actions to take."

If that's true, a strategic marketer evaluating current conditions would naturally ask (with an open mind for genuine illumination), "How did this crack team of business experts lose the battle for marketshare so badly under his rein?" Less than half of the cars sold in the US in 2008 were sold by GM, Ford, and Chrysler. It was the first time the US was dominated by the Asian and European car companies. The US companies held over two-thirds of the American market just eight years ago. If they knew the market, and the business, and had the talent to compete – why are they behind in meaningful product introductions? Where has this experience and knowledge Mr. Wagoner expected Americans to trust been demonstrated? How has it been proven?

The CEO's of the Big Three are all US born. They grew up in the United States and were educated in the United States. They live in American communities, with American neighbors, doing American things. Their core values, lifestyle, and culture are the values, lifestyles, and cultures engrained in every red-blooded American. These three men join us at the baseball park on Opening Day, are among us as we watch the fireworks on The Fourth of July, and carve the same traditional turkey on Thanksgiving. Yet, every day since taking the helm of their companies they have surrendered your business to people who were raised, educated, and live in places like Japan, Germany and South Korea.

Since the 1960's, Toyota, Nissan, and Honda have worked a planning process that forces them to understand the conditions of our marketplace and that identifies the evolving key success factors. They can't rely on assumptions and hunches about us, because their culture is so different from ours. They learn about us, our marketplace, and know our strengths and weaknesses. Focusing on specific needs and wants of the American consumer, they successfully meld qualities and features into products that address the complex factors associated with an automobile buying decision. They understand a car needs to be practical and fashionable, utilitarian but also ego-fulfilling. They see product gaps and fill them. For thirty years, they have been ahead of the US in meaningful, consumer-focused innovations.

The foreign producers focused on quality when the highly-compensated US workforce would ship anything to a dealer that resembled an automobile. Fit and finish were less important than the union's next collective bargaining agreement. For four decades, Toyota and others from beyond our shores systematically migrated into our driveways by employing purposeful tactics that were sure to generate success. The management in Japan knew we'd buy Toyota Corollas *en mass* here in

The United States. They know we'll buy Prius hybrids. Their planning processes told them. Are they quaking with fear knowing that Ford is coming after the "green" market? Does Ford have the market intelligence to even raise their concern?

As the leaders of the Big Three get giddy thinking about The Volt and an array of new hybrids, it still stands that these automakers are shutting down factories because the Japanese sell the core of the US population too many cars. Said more succinctly, the guys that run these three companies haven't produced what most of their neighbors want. Do the vehicles that they promise now battle against this statistical fact?

The reality of the American automobile crisis is that the practices and habits that are pulling them toward oblivion are based on a 90-year-old model for doing business that for forty years has been undoing them. There is no comprehensive strategic direction that positions their strengths and neutralizes their threats. They want to sell more cars, but they only have the imagination to apply tactics that have cultivated wearisome consumers. Discounts and bigger discounts. No interest loans. Employee pricing. These tactics all reinforce the notion that no American car will sell unless there is an image depreciating "deal" associated. What is the plan for American cars to sell at the sticker price on their own merits? How will they combat the fact that the resale value of a foreign car is greater than a Detroit vehicle? Perceived values are translated into the selling price. The price reflects the quality positioning in the consumer's mind.

There are more questions and doubt, than answers and assurances. Fifty independent automobile journalists voted Hyundai as the best car in North America in 2009. What will Chrysler put on the showroom floor to knock it off its pedestal? What is the plan to neutralize emerging competition from China and the consumer momentum for South Korean manufactured cars? As odd as it seems, the people who run the companies not located in the United States understand more about the American's relationship with the automobile. They understand the psychology of the consumer and the points to address that deliver the intangible "pride of ownership." What is the Big Three's plan to win the hearts of the next generation of consumers that have grown very accustomed to buying a wide range of products from China with confidence and pride? What will appeal to these consumers?

Among the problems contributing to the CEO's disconnection from the consumers they are charged to serve, is that their compensation has historically insulated them from the results they produce. In 1992, the compensation of the Big Three CEO's totaled $5.3 million for delivering $7.5 billion in losses. In 2007, GM and Ford's CEO's were paid $36 million in total compensation for $56 billion in losses. There's no personal investment of the leaders associated with such out-of-whack incentive programs.

Put in a different perspective, if the Philadelphia Phillies paid $18 million a season to a slugger for run production, he better be able to hit the ball out of the park or the "boos" would run him out of town. In a much more serious situation where the stakes involve the lives of hundreds-of-thousands of employees, the well-being of their suppliers, the portfolios and retirement nest eggs of shareholders, and the communities that have relied on the factories for their stability, to pay such obscene money for no good result is not defendable.

Alfred P. Sloan's model for running a business from the "top down" is obsolete in a competitive environment. It creates a culture where Henry Ford II would fire the bearer of new ideas and innovation. It generates the dangerous hubris born from a false level of comfort that believes experience has a bankable value. It isolates itself from the consumer. The leaders of The Big Three, equipped with an antiquated business model, stood before the American citizens as victims of labor, banking, and the unfair trade advantages of their foreign competitors. They are in a war, but they do not speak like warriors. They haven't adequately shared their plan to stand at the top of the mountain with the entreaty, "If you can find a better car, buy it." They come with a history that naturally begs asking how they will anticipate the changing currents of the markets where they must survive. What is the strategy to win? Until they have one, they will continue to lose.

After Congress scolded these three CEO's for such terrible performance, Wagoner stepped forward and volunteered to work for free. But that isn't the point. His salary is insignificant in the context of the big picture survival needs of GM. There is no pedantic expense control or some moral and ethical balance between performance and compensation that can shift the tide in GM's favor. If he hasn't succeeded in the past, he won't get any smarter with less income. These companies will get smarter by setting their course against a solid strategic plan that anticipates instead of reacts, that focuses on greatness and not gimmicks, and that passes the competition instead of follows the competition. When they start learning why people don't buy their cars and won't trust their brands, they will raise the corporate IQ of their company. When they start addressing these consumer's needs with appealing products that deliver value and quality, they will be on their way toward regaining leadership. They need to understand how the Japanese leaders plan. They need to figure out why a CEO living on the other side of the globe knows their customer's wants better than they do. They need to compete to win. They need to change to compete.

It has been proven by the Japanese in the US market. It is confirmed by Brother International's success. It is evidenced by the toothpaste you use and the cereal you eat. The war for marketshare can be won in the planning, and it can be lost as a result of a company's culture.

THE GAP BETWEEN KNOWING AND KNOWLEDGE

Getting to the kind of truth you can depend on for planning requires flexibility and an open mind for change. I once attended a business management retreat in which we participated in an exercise to prove another related (and very important) point. To complicate the importance of understanding the market, and your potential consumers, is the unsettling reality that different people with the same information may not interpret it the same way you do.

The little experiment impressed me. At the beginning, the twenty-five people that attended the retreat were split up into five diverse groups of five members. Each group received a sheet of paper with the personal "life situation" profiles of nine different individuals. They ranged from an executive vying for a seat in the US Senate, to a welfare mother with seven children. There was a doctor, a college professor and several community advocates. They ranged from nineteen to forty-five years old and included the spectrum of race and religious affiliations. Each had a compelling and valuable purpose for their life here on earth. Their only similarity was that they suffered from a terminal disease for which there was only one treatment, a specially designed one-of-a-kind mechanical kidney replacement.

In the instruction for this experiment, we learned that every candidate for the treatment was screened by doctors and had an equal opportunity for success. We were asked to choose who would live. Our selection had to be purposeful and based on an argument that supported our selection. Who do we save? It was a complex problem that combined moral, ethical, and practical aspects.

You could assume that a business management retreat would appeal to a group of people with a lot in common. They would have similar educational backgrounds and like ambitions. They would probably share a similar socio-economic profile. Their personal daily habits could be understandably interchangeable. Yet, from the five groups of five people and the nine possible answers, no group's members agreed unanimously to save the same person. Only two groups had the same solution. The exercise proved that the way we think, the things we know, and our cultural, moral and ethical influences shape us to be different from each other. The profoundness of this lesson is that what you and I think personally has no standing in setting the strategy for a company or product.

Nothing ever sold successfully because it appealed to the people selling it. Just because we think a product or a promotional campaign is a good idea behind the closed door of the conference room, it doesn't mean anyone beyond the door will buy it. I know all of the people at the business retreat believed, some very passionately, that they had the right answer when deciding which one of the inflicted would get the cure. Consider the lesson of this exercise as you set your marketing plan. Who among your customers or prospects cares what you or I think as they kick the tires of their next automobile purchase, buy their next insurance policy, or sit down for dinner at the convenient fast food restaurant? Our personal experiences or beliefs are no prediction for what anyone will buy.

When we understand the complexity of this simple truth, we allow ourselves to realize that the strategic planning of a business can be dangerous if done through a linear decision making process. To be overly impressed by your innovation and brilliance is meaningless to the ultimate consumer. To pull from past experiences and say, "This worked last year. Let's do it again," doesn't test or examine the decisions we make against the dynamic realities of where and when we do business. For example, during periods of prosperity, a full-blown advertising campaign that offers "employee pricing" and zero-percent financing to anyone considering the purchase of a new car, might sell more cars. When people are afraid of losing their jobs, when credit is difficult to come by, and when the product does not meet the wants of the available consumers, there can't be any assurance that spending for advertising could possibly produce an upward sales spike to even justify the cost of the ad. Same tactic, different current conditions, and a much different outcome.

It is worth remembering that we can know the facts, yet we can be in denial about (or purposefully ignore) others that may influence them. Like my airplane aisle-mate mentioned earlier in the book, justifying the move of his corporate headquarters, finding data to prove a preferred conclusion avoided the process that raises the questions that should have been asked. Among the most dangerous human tendencies is to refuse the facts that complete the picture, simply because what the picture looks like when they are included isn't ideally appealing. In short, one of our human qualities is to believe what we want to believe and disregard what we don't. It wouldn't be unusual to find passionate arguments for every wrong decision made at your business that are based on the limited facts the advocates are willing to accept.

On the other hand, there may be some alert individuals in a company who may see changes coming in the competitive marketplace that could bring either trouble or new opportunities. These people might suggest ideas to grow revenue or neutralize potential harm. But when their verified facts and substantiated recommendations are regularly dismissed, eventually these messengers with the unwelcome information realize they are actually creating problems for themselves professionally. They stop suggesting changes that could help the company better adapt to its dynamic market. They realize their discoveries are unwelcome.

When we are personally invested in anything, it is hard to see it with an undistorted view. Ask a coach of youth sports team about how distorted a parent's view of their child's abilities can be. "Why aren't you playing my kid?" The safe answer is usually some song and dance routine that helps defuse the parent's ire while still keeping the team competitive. Almost never will the coach give a truthful answer ("Because your kid is terrible"). The parent and the coach are watching the same things, but the parent is hopefully forgiving of their child's weaknesses and the coach can't afford to be.

So, extend the human trait that helps a youth sports coach soften the truth when talking to a parent about an untalented kid, to the business where one works, provides for their families, and finds their personal worth and validation. People in businesses lie to each other all of the time. Customers lie to their sales agents, sales agents lie to their bosses. The supervisors and managers throughout the company lie up and down the chain-of-command all day long. To say that you haven't ever reshaped the truth when delivering a potentially unpleasant nugget of news to a boss would be a lie. Sometimes it's to keep peace. Sometimes to earn a favor. Sometimes to stay employed. Sometimes the lies are even harmless. It isn't uncommon for a company to lie to itself and begin to take its most loyal consumers for granted. That could lead them to forget that each one of their customers comes back with regularity because the company has been able to best address their needs and wants. It forgets that the customer always has an eye open for something better.

Small businesses and huge global enterprises have been undone more regularly by ego and myopic arrogance than by any competitive pressure or market change. Some employees might see it as loyalty to never question the decisions being made within a company. Some may fear losing their job if they raise unwelcome concerns. Formal strategic planning provides the ideal tool for neutralizing an internal culture that could risk taking a path toward a company's destruction. Setting the right goals, answering the right questions, positioning a company for success, and then executing a series of tactics to generate business growth is the imperative of a formal strategic marketing plan.

Often, when conditions change within a market, the tendency of many business leaders is to "dig in" and do more of what made them successful in the past. There is a certain level of denial and an expectation that the problems can be fixed without fundamental changes within the organization. It wasn't uncommon in the 1970's to see stickers affixed to the bumpers of cars and trucks with "buy American" messages that slurred the foreign producers. With shift reductions and layoffs at the factories, the manufacturers and unions pointed the blame for the industrial slide on the consumer, charging that "buying foreign" wasn't patriotic. The truth, however, was that toward the end of the 1960's, the Japanese came to our shores, saw vulnerabilities in the US auto producer's product lines and labor structure, and launched an economic war they were positioned to win. They raised consumer expectations. They may have influenced the improvement of American cars, but today the same foreign producers are still better prepared and the reward for satisfying the consumer is shifting even further away from Detroit.

By now, hopefully we all know that the automobiles Americans prefer to drive have nothing to do with the patriotism of the consumer. In fact, in the free market, buying the best available value is the patriot's duty. It is supposed to be competitive pressures that drive innovation and force us past mediocrity. The American system demands that the competition push itself to improve and evolve. If anything, the lack of patriotism in America comes from the top of the industries and labor unions that failed to realize that the American people shouldn't be taken for granted or underestimated. They offended the US consumer and weakened our country by not delivering products, qualities, and values that Americans would become accustomed to (and comfortable buying) from the foreign producers. They failed to go to war to protect our economic and cultural survival. It wasn't just cars. Japan defined the competition for home entertainment, consumer electronics, office machines, and other product categories.

In every strata of American business, it's time to pull our heads out from wherever we have them hidden, look at the truth, and start competing again. The consumer makes the rules. It's time for US business leaders to start winning them over with American ingenuity and the innovations brought from an educated US workforce. That isn't going to happen by lobbying Congress for softer regulations and stricter trade restrictions on the importers. That is going to take a workable strategic plan – not a government bailout.

Frequently, there are easy ways that present themselves that will produce short-term prosperity. It's possible to be successful by foregoing a strict plan and pushing forward with a hunch. Yet, when we take a strategic approach that evaluates every element of a problem to produce the best opportunities, we make sure we don't overlook hidden possibilities. Perhaps it is just a coincidence, but the most successful strategic business planners I have known were educated first as scientists and engineers. Maybe it is simply because these disciplines attract higher IQ's. I tend to believe it is because scientists systematically look past the obvious, test their assumptions, and track their results to reveal new frontiers.

There's a frequently told story about NASA. It's a "can't see the forest for the trees" tale about the investment made to develop a ball point pen that would work in the zero-gravity environs of space. As the story is told, NASA invested valuable scientific talent and money to solve the problem. Meanwhile, the space agency in the Soviet Union looked at the same problem and decided to use pencils.

When this story is repeated, it always is done at the expense of NASA engineers. How could such an obvious solution be overlooked by the folks that won the race to the moon? One might think it's unimaginable that the most prestigious science agency in the world could miss the solution that any nine-year-old could suggest. So, let's suppose they didn't. Maybe "How did they overlook the obvious?" isn't the right question to ask. Maybe the question to ask is, "What opportunities did they create?"

Marketing is the art of acting on opportunities in capitalism. It's often said that "necessity is the mother of invention." Yet, for a strategic mind, this is backward thinking. In forward thinking companies "opportunity" is the mother of invention. An obvious response to an immediate necessity may be the correct one, yet sometimes it can obfuscate a larger, long-term opportunity. In the USSR they just wanted to answer how to make a written record in space. In the USA the question was "How do we get the pen to work without gravity?" NASA looked for a solution past the pencil because they weren't communists.

Perhaps a NASA engineer taking the morning train to his office may have noticed a man standing against the handrail shaking the ink of his Bic down to the tip so he could finish the last few squares of the morning crossword puzzle. In the stall of a public restroom he might have taken note that the prose inked above the paper roller starts in bold blue ink but fades before the punch line. Maybe he had experienced the frustration of pulling a mechanical pencil from his breast pocket to jot a quick note, only to have the lead snap as quickly as his thumb could advance it forward.

In the free enterprise system, technological breakthroughs and innovation are rewarded. For NASA, a pen that worked in a zero-gravity environment would be more favorable than using a pencil for a range of reasons including waste management, the permanence of the records, and product lifespan. The breakthroughs in developing a pen that worked in weightlessness could have further implications in fluid management in space or even supersonic flight. More meaningful was recognizing the potential commercial implications of a "space-aged" zero-gravity pen. In the socialism of Soviet Russia, one could say it wasn't genius at all that suggested a pencil to answer the question of "How can we write in space?" They simply failed to see past the obvious because their scientists were not influenced by the commercial prospects of the problem.

Building a working strategy requires a specific kind of thinking, whether it is filling empty seats for a professional hockey team, penetrating the office products channel with more goods, or increasing revenue as a wholesale distributor. Marketing is not about "doing something," it is about "doing the right thing." To do the right thing you need to apply a strategic solution that goes to the root of each problem. Like the innovative NASA solution to writing in space, how a problem is pondered determines how it will be resolved.

As a society, America has become enamored with a canned "how to" mentality. There's a "12 step" plan for everything from building real estate wealth, raising children, losing weight, and even writing better sentences. The culture is flooded with books promising the paint-by-numbers, connect-the-dots answer to any problem imaginable. There's a book that will teach you how to master both business and life within one week if you have an hour to spare each day. Unfortunately, successful marketing is not so easy.

The classic format for strategic marketing does not give you the answers, but it can lead you to them. It has specific elements that must be followed, but they should never be considered in the mechanical mindset that creates strategy by filling in the blanks. The strategic planning process is a format for uncovering the total potential of an organization. If done correctly, it is a process that solves problems by helping you find the right questions. It is a framework for thinking. The way we think influences how problems are approached.

There are four basic types of thinking processes that those responsible for their company's security must be aware of: intuitive, mechanical, linear, and strategic. Being able to understand where your advice is coming from helps to weigh its value.

Intuitive thinkers see a problem and focus on individual solutions. They will act on experience and educated "hunches" that quite often can be successful in answering the question. An intuitive thinker might answer the question about how to increase attendance at a hockey game by suggesting "theme nights" to sell seats to community organizations or company employees. "I have a feeling that if we have a Student Night, we'll draw more students." Following intuition is effective only in a static environment where hunches based on experience are valid.

Mechanical thinkers may look at the elements available and suggest a solution to the problem through their rearrangement. For example, you have tickets to sell, and because those ticket holders need to park their car, it makes sense that adding a special ticket package with a parking incentive will add ticket sales. Families with budget concerns will respond to a family night with special bargains on food concessions and other incentives. An intuitive thinker, working with a mechanical thinker, might suggest that a hockey fan is typically a beer drinking male and that a "50 cent" beer night has natural appeal to that segment. These are all ideas that could incrementally add seat sales. The problem with this kind of approach is that it is hard to know what the real impact might be. They also could just erode the profit margins that could have produced effective promotions to expand the loyal fan base.

Although the mechanical and intuitive solutions could add attendance, neither of these addresses the real problem. Does free parking or cheap beer really cultivate new fans? Does the increase in individual ticket sales for one night recover the losses in parking or concession revenue? Will it create a new value expectation that can't be sustained profitably? This needs to be determined. Based on attendance at games for Tier II teams in minor league hockey across the continent, the accepted gimmicks for selling seats are not working to add long-term value to the enterprise. Attendance for any minor league sports team rarely grows over time. But in some pockets, there is a great consumer loyalty and a solid record of sell outs. These are organizations with a strategic-minded solution.

A strategic thinker would hear the question, "How do we increase attendance?" and isolate the character of each critical element of the problem. To the strategic thinker, the real puzzle to solve is "Why does the question have to be asked in the first place?" A strategic thinker would hear the solutions of the intuitive and mechanical thinkers, and then ask if they address the critical elements of the problem. A critical strategic thinker would think with fiduciary responsibility about the resources invested to sell the seats and would adapt ways to measure results against projected outcomes. Who will this draw? Thinking mechanically and intuitively, one can come to a solution that produces a result. But does the result address the strategic goals of the franchise? How to sell more tickets is an obvious question. The less obvious question is, "Why don't we have more fans?"

Most commonly, business planning at companies takes a linear approach. Having a linear approach in the 1950's and 60's, the leaders of the century-old Studebaker brand proved that there's no guarantee that the age of a company ensures its survival. Things had gone reasonably well for over one-hundred years, only to see a few seemingly practical decisions change things forever.

In the early 1960's, Studebaker was a company whose history stretched back to building horse-drawn wagons in the 1850's. Just before their demise they seemed to be on the verge of some very good decisions. The automobile market was bigger than any time in history. Their cars, on so many counts, were peerless in performance and innovation. Like many companies, Studebaker had chances to make some decisions that, with just very small variations, may have stabilized their future. Taken to the verge of greatness they opted with regularity to miss the opportunity. But it's not as if they were not a bumbling wreck of incompetence.

Studebaker had a culture of innovation. They were the first to introduce windshield defoggers, windshield washers, and air conditioning. Studebaker pioneered the dash-mounted fuel gauge. The innovative "Hill Holder" clutch found on the Subaru Forrester after 2003 was first seen on Studebaker Presidents in 1936, where it was also called the Hill Holder. In the US, disk brakes were first sold as a standard item on Studebaker automobiles. The company had a century of marketing "firsts." Considering everything Studebaker had going for it, this was a brand considerably ahead of its time.

In 1939, Studebaker had established a strong consumer position and grabbed a significant share of the market with the introduction of the Champion. The Champion was a frame-up innovation that became the lightweight economy leader to address the consumer needs of the gas-rationing period of World War II. The basic model could be bought for $660. Affordable, economical, and sporty, the model held a strong position into the 1950's. Like many companies enjoying success, Studebaker's vision for the future failed to see the vulnerabilities that lay ahead for them.

The South Bend, Indiana factory never experienced a strike. The company maintained concessionary relations with the labor unions and in 1950 they had the highest paid workers of all automobile manufacturers. Their pension obligation was the highest per employee. The manpower overhead required that the company generate strong unit sales, profits and cash flow. Unfortunately, at an inopportune time, Studebaker experienced a brief period of quality problems.

In the early 1950's, GM and Ford were battling in a vicious price war that ultimately redefined the order of the industry. Weaker brands disappeared. The combination of internal and external pressures sent Studebaker into receivership.

During this period, Studebaker merged with Packard to add a prestige nameplate to their product line up. They became the Studebaker-Packard Corporation. Prior to completing the merger, Packard's management didn't realize the depth of Studebaker's financial problems. To deal swiftly with these woes, a financially-focused management team was brought in from the Curtiss-Wright aircraft maker to set the company on a new course. The financial experts guided the company under the blanket of bankruptcy, abandoning long-term vision in favor of short-term gains. Directed by the quick fixes initiated by their financial vision, they began taking a series of actions that would have been hard to disagree with at the time.

They closed the Packard factory. They bolted Studebaker power plants under the Packard hood. They shared body panels with the Studebaker President. With nothing but a nameplate and trim to distinguish the models, they pushed forward with ignorance of the automobile consumer's psyche. Loyal Packard owners recognized that the difference between a Studebaker and a Packard was deeper than body panels and trim embellishments. Studebaker quickly lost their Packard customers and the dealer base soon followed. They had a great idea on paper for bringing more efficient returns to the company's bottom line. They also broke the promise of the Packard brand.

Toward the end of the decade the Studebaker brand began showing a lot of promise. The introduction of the 1959 Lark made "second car" ownership accessible to a wider range of middle class Americans. The Lark was among the first "compact" cars addressing a niche unmet by Detroit. Larks offered value, economy, and affordability. It was a niche that delivered an answer to the company's financial strife. With a product that addressed an unsaturated market, they needed to strike quickly.

The company moved swiftly to execute their aggressive distribution strategy, positioning the Lark on the showroom floors of the established dealers of the Big Three auto brands. All across the country The Lark addressed a product gap that the auto retailers of the leading brands were happy to let Studebaker fill. Innovative and affordable, the emerging two-car family gravitated to the brand. In 1959 and 1960 the Lark enjoyed brisk sales by tapping into the traffic brought on the backs of the promotional efforts and branding strength of the larger competitors.

This success however, came abruptly to a stop a few years later when every Detroit brand introduced a direct competitor for the Lark. The Big Three demanded dealers terminate their relationship with Studebaker. That market was lost more quickly than it was gained. In hindsight, the short-term mentality of Studebaker marketing cultivated the compact segment and then delivered it to the showrooms of industry's biggest and strongest brands, setting the table perfectly for their Chevy II, Falcon, and Dart products. By tagging along with the bigger companies' distribution networks, the Studebaker brand took a back seat to the competitors' strengths.

A forward long-range thinking Studebaker might have expected that the market-leaders wouldn't stand idle and allow their franchises to pedal Studebakers. They would have drafted a strong plan to hold onto the compact car market they established. Instead, with the brand exiled from the showrooms where they once sold swiftly, Studebaker's image was left to the salesperson who would explain that "we did carry Studebaker, but now we have this Falcon. Wouldn't you rather have a Ford?"

Studebaker may have been on the cusp of greatness. In the car-crazy 1950's and 60's Americans fell in love with motor sports. NASCAR, the Indy 500, and the quarter-mile drag strips across America made auto racing the fastest growing spectator sport in the country, second only to horse racing. The "Big Three," General Motors, Ford, and Chrysler, all supported motor sports in the 1950's and 60's as an effective and important element of their market-building strategy. "Win on Sunday, sell on Monday" was a common expression bantered on their car lots.

Studebakers were relevant in performance motor sports, too, but in obscure arenas that lacked the attention and romance of USAC, NASCAR, and NHRA. You could find the circa-1950 Studebakers as favorites among the Salt Flats land speed record-setters in Utah. The 1963 Avanti laid claim to being "The Fastest Production Car in America," setting twenty-nine different national stock car records in twelve hours. Andy Granitelli set land speed records for production passenger cars when he took a totally stock supercharged Studebaker Hawk and Lark to speeds of 140 and 132 miles per hour. To the media and consumers, these achievements lacked the sensation that was associated with flexing power against a worthy opponent on the quarter-mile drag strip, the rolling hills of Sebring, or the ovals of NASCAR.

Studebaker's achievements didn't capture the same romantic appeal that rubbing the paint off the fenders of the other brands at Darlington did. There was none of the gladiator bravery associated with these feats. It lacked the primitive appeal of the chariot race. They only took boring minutes to achieve and had few thrills to sustain the audience necessary to sell beer and laundry soap on the television networks.

Dollar-for-dollar, in 1962 no brand offered consumers the power and performance of the Studebaker. The Super Hawk featured a supercharged motor with a 140 MPH top speed and the industry's first "twin traction" differential to push the car out of any snow bank. It had a power-to-weight ratio only bested by the expensive Chrysler 300 during the 1960's. In every measurable way the cars met the needs and wants of significant market segments. But there was a problem in how the Studebaker brand was parked in the minds of the consumers. Since 1939, regardless of their century of innovation and performance achievement, in the minds of car buyers they were the "lightweight and easy on the budget" automobile brand.

In 1957, Studebaker marketed the Hawk series as "family sports cars," to which the August 1957 issue of *Motor Life* said was "probably as good a description as any." What does such a description mean? How does it fit into the psyche of the sports car consumer? How did it appeal to the guy looking to buy the family car? A sports car is a symbol of individualism. A family car was a bore.

Pound-for-pound, in 1963 the Super Hawk was the most powerful passenger sports car you could buy. It is considered by many to be the precursor of the "muscle cars" produced by the Detroit brands later in the decade. It had a back seat and adequate trunk space so that it could appeal to the "family" market. The Hawk was the only game in town that offered performance and room for the groceries. Yet, "Family Sports Car" for a performance coupe was as appealing as a "Clothes for Fat Kids" sign that you'd never see at the local JC Penney to describe the husky boy department. It describes what it is, but it doesn't promote the image that the consumer wants positioned in their mind.

Before the dust could settle from the Hawk's introduction and demise, the Big Three rolled out Mustangs, Camaros, and 'Cudas on to their showroom floors. These models would be seen at the curbs of suburban split-level homes. Adolescent boys would cup their hands against the glass to peek inside to see if they had Hurst four-speeds or automatics. They checked the speedometers for their maximum MPH number as if the dashboard represented what was possible from the power under the hood. Moms and dads hopped in them to take kids to school, to grab the guys in the car pool, or to make the Wednesday trip to the grocery store. But, these were not family cars.

How big was the market that bought "family sports cars?" In 1962 it was less than 8,400. In 1963 it was 4,000. The next year, the market was saturated with less than 2,000 Hawks sold before the model was tossed on the scrap heap with other un-saleable models. With the Hawk, Studebaker did a great job of creating a car to address the performance market. Yet, their public relations and press missed the mark, their distribution was unstable, and the model was doomed even before it got a chance.

It's tragic to consider this misstep against the fertile market that was actually available when Hawks were rolling off the assembly line. The 8,400 units sold in 1962 didn't scratch the potential. In the first three years of the Mustang, Ford produced 1.5 million automobiles on a body bolted to a Falcon frame. Was the four-passenger, 283 cubic inch V-8 Mustang a "family sports car?" It fit the description Studebaker gave the Hawk. But "Pony Car" was much more appealing to the ego of the consumers drawn to the Mustang.

As the next years rolled along, the Studebaker brand became diluted by a range of confusing and unsettling decisions. The factory in South Bend, Indiana was shut down and all production moved to Canada where Studebaker previously made only trucks. The car's power-plants were being bought from Chevy in the US to replace the Studebaker engines. "Common Sense Car" ads appeared in magazines sharing space with the emerging Volkswagen brand (a partnership in advertising born from the fact Studebaker of Canada, Ltd was that country's importer of Volkswagen). This may have been a cheaper print campaign but the ads didn't register positive or measurable results.

The actions and activities of Studebaker in its last years were flawed. Keen research of market conditions would have packaged the image of the products to more palatably appeal to the "hot buttons" of the targeted consumers. Studebaker's actions to save itself demonstrate the kind of thinking that might follow a strict linear and mechanical financial management mentality. A company cannot isolate themselves from their competitors, markets, or consumers. They must always know to whom they are selling. They must anticipate the market. They must get inside the heads of their consumers to understand them as personally as possible. They must establish sustainable distribution and provide reliable customer support. Short-term tactics must only be a component of a long-term plan.

Of course, hindsight makes experts. Ride the time machine backwards. So much of what was done to save the company seemed to make brilliant sense. Put yourself in the Studebaker President's office in 1959. How would you have acted? What would you recommend? Could you disagree with the plans put on the table for short-term gains?

With the 1959 Lark, it was simple and efficient to convince an established Dodge dealer that there's a niche market he is missing by not having Studebaker models on his showroom floor. Could you have seen the risks against what may have sounded very attractive in the static environment? By shutting down the Packard plant, the revenue the brand was generating would show an impressive bottom-line improvement brought by savings in manpower, facility overhead, inventory efficiencies, and improved cash-flow. It was easy to understand that a "family sports car" would appeal to a large segment of the "40-somethings" of the 1960's. Knowing what to do in real time is always harder than knowing what should have been done. In a static time frame and the paradigm of business in South Bend, these were examples of wisdom. In a vacuum, these are sound, solid business decisions. The moral is this: You can run your business any way you want if it is in a vacuum.

The problem with many unsuccessful organizations is that their solutions are internally focused. At Studebaker in 1959 they built a car that consumers wanted. It was an intuitive thinker that set the plan to use the leading Big-Three retailers to get the swift penetration they needed. It was the mechanical thinker that shut down the Packard plant to lower operating costs. It was a linear thinker that thought youthful auto enthusiasts with families would buy a "family sports car." A more strategically focused plan might have solved well-defined challenges that fit the vision of the long-range future of the company. It would have been drafted in the context of addressing the needs and wants of consumers.

This 100-year-old company didn't fade away. They fought hard trying to solve one problem at a time so that they could survive another day. Sometimes that seems to be the only way for a company that is struggling to make it – persevering with a plan that makes sense and solves the problems at hand. Unfortunately, when the actions fail to position all of an entity's strengths so they fit successfully within the dynamic conditions of the market and its evolution over time, the consequences can be dire.

Like many companies, Studebaker had great ideas. They just did a bad job ensuring that these ideas, in the short-term, would not harm the company by being out-of-step with a longer range vision. They knew what to do, and took actions based on experience and current conditions. Yet, they cultivated no knowledge that helped them understand the consequences of their decisions.

PLANNING TO BE VULNERABLE

Years ago, while consulting for a handful of minor league ice hockey organizations, I was told of a conversation between two team owners. "My team has been the league champion for the last three years," one of the men said. "Why can't I make money?" It was the perfect question to illustrate that many aren't sure enough about their businesses, or the opportunities within the markets they serve, to produce success. Discussing strategic marketing in the context of the secondary-market minor league ice hockey industry is worthwhile because what most think would be the obvious path to prosperity, isn't.

Conventional sports marketing wisdom would lead one to think that it didn't make sense that this team struggled financially. The successful formula in premier leagues like Major League Baseball, the NFL, the NBA, and the NHL includes showcasing standout athletes and packing stadiums by winning championships. Yet, in major sports leagues the markets are huge and the consumer targeting can be highly focused, excluding anyone but fans of their sport. The advantage of marketing a sport in a major city is that there is usually such a significant population that you can depend upon devoted fans alone to fill the seats at games. The minor league team's General Manager might believe that the tactics that work in the big league could be transferable to his smaller town's franchise. Nothing could be less true.

Minor league ice hockey clubs expose many of the unique challenges that serve as examples to anyone charged with planning their enterprise's fortunes in any industry. It is impossible to know whether what will work in one market translates into a smart strategy for another without specific market knowledge. For example, the major market National Hockey League profile for the hockey fan is a white, middle-aged, college-educated professional. If you move from Detroit as an assistant in the marketing department of the NHL Red Wings to the minor league team in Fort Wayne to take the helm, you need to know that only a few of the techniques learned in the previous job may work to meet your attendance goals. While Joe Lewis Arena can be sold-out by targeting mostly affluent middle-aged white men, it is also important to realize that in 2005 the team that had gained the greatest percentage of its available population in all of professional hockey drew primarily an ethnically Mexican population, with very moderate incomes, who live along the border of the Rio Grande. The balance of the marketing mix in Detroit is not going to be the same as it is in Fort Wayne or El Paso.

In minor league sports, cultivating meaningful fans from the market becomes almost infinitely more challenging due to the shear fact that the smaller markets lack the critical mass necessary to narrowly target. Mistakes and misjudgments carry a higher toll. In Philadelphia it takes 0.035% of the population to fill the 18,000 seat arena. In 2005, Columbus, Georgia's team drew nearly 1.000% of their available population to every game, but still left their 7,509 seat arena 75% empty. In terms of available market success, they far outperformed most teams in every level of hockey. To draw one-percent of the population, the team had to cultivate a following from an audience bigger than the town's devoted hockey fans, with a product that appealed to the broadness of the community.

Bernard Baruch, a Wall Street genius in the early 1900's and the economic advisor to Democratic Presidents Woodrow Wilson and Franklin D. Roosevelt said, "If you get all the facts, your judgments can be right. If you don't get all the facts, they can't be right." Paraphrased in the simplest terms, the key to making any successful plan – whether you are a coach or a business manager - is to get past any distractions, obfuscations, emotional slants, prejudices, or myths and to confine all decisions to those that are based on facts which are known, verified, and tested. It's the premise behind enduring brands and companies. It is also the cornerstone of every successful coach's philosophy. In fact, the habits of successful coaches provide the perfect example for how strategic business planning should be approached.

To win a championship, a coach builds a comprehensive strategy for success. The strategy evaluates the competitors. It learns everything possible about the various fields of play in which they will be competing. It highlights the key factors necessary to be successful. Certainly there are risks that are taken, but the risks are measured against probabilities. Each decision is in balance with the possible short-term-gain and the team's longer-term objectives. With the only prospects of the game's outcome being a win, a loss, or a tie, the coaching staff works intensely to make the team as competitive as possible. They realize their absolute vulnerability and strive to take nothing for granted.

In a quest for winning championships, a sports team's strategic planning involves gathering information that measures the talent of the opposing players and studies the game tendencies of the opposing coaches. Players and staff are carefully chosen to add specialized understandings of every facet of the game. Schemes and specific plays are developed to make the most of the available talent against the weaknesses of the opponent. There is a season-long strategy that puts together a championship structure. Tactics are adjusted for individual games. Everyone that influences the outcome is focused on the same things.

Week-by-week, coaches and players study film. They evaluate themselves and dissect the habits of the opponent. Mechanical flaws, bad habits, and mental errors are reviewed individually with players so they can make corrections and work at their very best. Coaches read injury reports and are very careful in how they report the injuries of their own team. It's a seven-day, never-ending effort to stay ahead of the opponent. It's necessary because in the competitive world of sports, knowledge is dynamic. What you know today may not be true tomorrow.

Winning consistently comes from both long and short-term preparation. When teams fail to win games it is usually because they don't have the necessary talent, the right plan, adequate scouting and recruiting, strong coaching, and/or commitment and focus. When games are won, it is because there was no aspect of the game overlooked or taken for granted. This is also the most sustaining and successful approach to business management.

Yet, in an irony that is impossible to miss, a sampling of the management practices in minor league hockey showed an almost complete absence of formal strategic planning. It also showed that most teams that do take a formal approach to strategic planning were among the few that actually sustained themselves profitably. The closer a team operated to the strategic marketing principles used in the consumer packaged goods industries, the more significant and enduring their success. The more their habits for growing their businesses mimicked the activities in the coach's office, the more likely they were to make money. Teams that planned knew more about their markets and responded with appropriate and cost effective promotions. They looked ahead to address pending threats preemptively.

In 2005, hockey's elite second tier minor league, the ECHL, boasted their growth and celebrated their enduring survival. Yet at the time, only one team from the original East Coast Hockey League had survived. "The league is growing" was the message from the ECHL in 2005. Yet, the growth that the league boasted as a measure of its sustaining success was gained though the absorption of another league and the dumping of some poorly performing organizations, not in the actual attendance numbers in each arena at the individual team level. The teams that were in the league prior to its West Coast expansion actually lost an average of nearly 150 fans per game.

The ECHL's public relations effort was selling a true fact, but not "all the facts" that the late Bernard Baruch said are critical to effective decision making. In 2005 the league boasted record attendance. The announcement gave owners a good feeling that obfuscated the reality that they were nearly all in a decline. In fact, attendance at ECHL games – even with the expansion – was consistent with the fact that after its first or second year a team's attendance turns downward.

In Tier II Minor League Hockey, a team rarely survives more than six seasons. But that comes as no surprise when you compare the work habits between the top executives' and the coaches' offices of many teams. A coach of a competitive team is always on the alert for opportunities and vulnerabilities because every contest between two foes is designed to produce a winner and a loser. Their critical need to gather information, evaluate conditions to determine what is necessary for success, and to set season-long strategies and specific game plans is obvious - at the end of the day at least half of the outcomes are not wins. No such mathematical restriction exists in the front office of the sports team. All teams could succeed financially. Yet, even with this unlimited potential for success, the majority of teams fail.

Often located just a few doors away from where coaches prepare to prevail in games, you'll find the business office. They are creative. They are experienced. Yet, based on the results they post, if understanding your consumer's needs is a basic marketing principle that makes one successful, then the majority of small market ice hockey teams must know little about their prospective customers. The business office fails to cultivate enough dependable revenue from the marketplace to sustain their enterprise. They fail in competing.

An extraordinary reality of small-market sports franchises is that the energy invested in putting together the most competitive team is virtually immaterial in producing seat sales. A team's record in minor league sports has little impact on attendance. As such, instead of budgeting for attractive coaching salaries and premium player contracts to build ice champions, an investment in finding managers with experience in consumer marketing might be more justified. From the practices I have observed, in cases where a community-presence for the franchise's brand and sustainable seat sales had been created, it has been directly related to having the right consumer-focused, market-aware business management in place. The leadership of any company is a key factor of success.

Many teams string gimmicks and spot promotions throughout the team's game schedule. These activities are intended to increase attendance. At the end of the year, most teams show fewer seats sold. Where did they go? Why did they leave? The General Managers of these teams can explain their losses but few can explain their efforts to prevent them. They work hard to replace their advertisers and sponsors. But, they don't do much to develop pointed strategic tactics to maintain and increase the kind of attendance that gives them an enduring and financially justifiable return. Thinking up the next promotion hasn't proven to be effective in solving the fundamental problem. Why don't these teams have more fans?

In 2005, while doing market research for a handful of minor league hockey teams, I discovered a standout organization located in Boise, Idaho. This ECHL hockey team worked from a formal strategic plan and had enjoyed consistent years of near sell-out attendance and annual profits. This fact put them in a very narrow class of teams that could be considered successful. They proved that the best chance for success comes to those that make the effort to accurately know their current conditions, correctly identify the key success factors, and set strategies and tactics with a high probability of achievement toward their identified goals. They also showed a stark contrast to the vision and attitude that leaves most teams doomed before their first ticket sale.

The Steelheads didn't cultivate seat sales on game day. The things they did from day-to-day were in the context of the longer vision of their strategic plan. Looking forward, the Idaho Steelheads recognized their sell-out status for the first eight years also was accompanied by an average age of the ticket holder increasing by almost eight years. Certainly, this statistic spoke well to the team's fan retention. But it also projected a problem that they needed to actively address. They realized a need to work beyond their sell-out attendance to get into the community with their brand to ensure they were cultivating a younger generation to replace the current ticket holders as they got older. They had a formal plan designed to preserve their future through the anticipated dynamics in the market. Again, it's unusual for a team to know this much about their committed fan base.

For any business - whether it is minor league hockey, selling toothpaste, or manufacturing automobiles - getting past assumptions, hunches, and experience can stimulate new possibilities and greater success. In minor league ice hockey (or any other business) the managers should not only know why people buy their product or service, but why qualified prospects don't. What are the benefits of the product? Do different segments get different benefits? What is it that makes some people committed repeat consumers and others indifferent? Which segments need to be cultivated to ensure success and how can they be secured? These answers cannot be decided by the owner, the general manager, or the marketing wiz in the confines of the office. Long-term success in a dynamic market requires practical and substantiated research, monitoring and measuring the actions taken against the expected achievement, and continued testing and challenging of the information on which all decisions are based.

I tried to have this discussion with a General Manager who had taken the reigns of a hockey team when its attendance was recorded at just below 7,000 per game. This was 2,000 seats less than the team enjoyed just a few years before and his mission was to turn things around. I suggested that he needed to know the consequences of every action his organization would take in terms of the impact on consumers he needed to attract and keep. He assured me he had a degree in sports marketing and was well-trained to act fearlessly. Being a financially-oriented manager, he immediately cut the generous "free ticket" distribution practices of his predecessor. In his first year he showed an increase in profit with an average attendance of 6,000 fans. Two years later they filled approximately 4,500 seats per game.

Like many people at the helms of companies, he felt that everything he needed to know was taught to him in school, gained through experience, or observed through the successes of others. He was certain and confident that his knowledge-base was all he needed to know in order to do what was best for the franchise. He told me that he was an expert in "sports marketing." He explained that this is a different discipline than "consumer marketing." He was making a case for the insignificance of the reported attendance decline during his first years at the helm. He talked about the growing competition for the consumer's dollars in his market and the changing demographics within the community. He didn't talk at all about changing the habits of his organization to address these conditions. This team's top executive may have misunderstood the depth of loyalty among season ticket holders and he may have taken the commercial advertisers for granted. He missed the fact that the fans expect more than a hockey game for their money.

Loyal fans that purchased season tickets ever since the first days when all the seats in the arena were filled, looked to the seats next to them and discovered they were empty on both sides. The roar that once sent tingles down their spines every time a great goal was scored became dramatically less powerful. The season ticket holders' positive experience with the brand was diminished, and many could no longer justify their ticket purchase commitment. Before executing tactics that could influence attendance, the General Manager should have understood how many filled seats will deliver the season ticket holder the entertainment value they expect. That's the core business worth protecting.

The General Manager wrongly expected his commercial sponsors would invest the same dollars to reach 2,000 fewer potential prospects. With a watch on the cost-per-impression of their advertising budgets, the sponsors were tempted to question the soundness of their investment. They'd also question the wisdom of associating their brand with a losing one. There's a point when the value they got from sponsoring the team wouldn't make sense anymore. How many more consumers could the corporate sponsor of a hockey team reach in his targeted demographic if he ran an ad in the newspaper instead? How much would each of those impressions cost? The deal they had for exposure to 7,000 fans becomes less valuable when only 4,500 come through the turnstiles.

Like the Curtiss-Wright team that came in to fix Studebaker, the soundness of the decisions by the General Manager of this sports franchise seemed crystal clear when he looked at the immediate measurements to gauge results. But in management, all decisions are intertwined and influence the ultimate long-term success of the franchise. The discipline generally required by proper strategic thinking prevents any actions without first having a vision for their consequences over time. The Steelheads also modified their complimentary ticket policies. Yet, their action plan replaced the occupants of these seats (that at one time didn't produce revenue) with ticket purchasing fans. Like the coach evaluating his roster and play options within the context of the team's championship aspirations, the action taken by the Steelheads did not risk changing the consumer's game enjoyment to post short-term gains. This brings us back to the initial point.

The General Manager in this story had an attitude that can be commonly found among managers of almost any kind of business. It's a head-in-the-sand approach that copies practices that don't work. A General Manager of a successful small market team in the Southern Professional Hockey League told me that his assistant once suggested a few tactics that had been used by the minor league basketball team he worked for a couple years before in the same town. He asked his assistant how well these ideas worked. Knowing that the minor league basketball team that used these tactics failed and folded, he wanted to know why his assistant thought they were a good idea.

The reason these ideas were suggested is that they had been used before, might have actually worked for somebody somewhere, are frequently repeated in other organizations, give that warm feeling that something is being done to grow the business, and fit in the comfort-zone of "sports marketing professionals." When teams begin doing what is accepted and comfortable, they are doomed. This is to say, based on the current conditions of the market, all minor league sports teams have little chance to survive without a fundamental departure from their comfort-zones.

There are several examples of well-managed minor league ice hockey teams. Yet, simply adopting the action plans of the few successful teams in order to address a revenue generation problem would result in a continuation of mistakes for most struggling teams. The marketing mix of successful teams in South Texas, Central Colorado, and Southern Idaho are very different and unique to the markets they serve.

The Idaho Steelheads of the ECHL through 2005 had bucked the trend of Tier II minor league hockey. The Steelheads posted a profit and achieved a steady history of near-sell-out attendance. The team's payroll is far above the average in the industry. The breadth of their staff's consumer marketing experience is wider. As part of their plan, they reached into the marketplace and meaningfully developed an image that goes beyond the hockey fans who attend games. Part of their written strategy includes specific tactics to engrain the brand into the fabric of the community.

The Steelheads in Idaho worked from a process that is shared by the majority of all leading consumer products, every major consumer brand, and every leading packaged-goods company with a sustained history of success. They have people in their front office with a consumer marketing background. They prove that if you are a butcher, a baker, or a candlestick maker, or the visionary of any business in any industry, that a strategic plan is the best foundation for survival. They thrive in an industry where revenue and attendance declines are accepted as "business as usual." Like all successful businesses, the Idaho Steelheads focus on very specific and sustainable tactics to systematically move toward measurable success. They not only sell a lot of tickets. They have found ways to link their brand to the community. Like the coach trying to win the season championship, the General Manager in Idaho knows that success is tied directly to the time and energy dedicated to planning.

A defunct team in Roanoke, Virginia used tough-guy billboard images and violent slogans to promote its product to the market. "Season's Beatings" a billboard said at Christmas. Their campaign strategy was woven together by negative images and inside jokes that might amuse a hockey fan defined by NHL research, that also were certain to fail in appealing to the wider breadth of consumers necessary to produce a sustained presence for a minor league team. They had a news columnist condemn them in the paper with disparaging press that might actually have been useful in drawing more hockey fans. But face it, how many hockey fans are going to be found in the mountains of Virginia? Their campaign was firmly justified by the well-known fact that violence is the primary appeal of the sport to 90% of hockey's fans. Yet, there is also a study showing that for over 90% of all women, violence is the single biggest road block to gaining their interest.

Equipped with the facts, we know that such a campaign may reflect the attributes of a game experience that appeal to those that manage the organization. But what appeals to the mother of three young children? Is there a better image that would attract the potential business client? How is the team segmenting their market in order to target a message that appeals to the needs of each customer profile? With a commitment to market research, a management organization may discover that the only blows delivered by a "Season's Beatings" billboard are to their fan attendance and advertising budget.

Being market-aware, the Idaho Steelheads announced a partnership with Gold's Gym that would bring a fitness message to school children, and by their effort, they have effectively taken valuable steps to cultivate their brand with the people who will eventually replace the current ticket purchasers that attribute to their steady string of full-capacity ticket sales for their venue. They focused on a positive impression that children would take home to moms and dads, adding to the demand from the broad base of their community's consumers. It was the kind of plan born from knowing.

The struggles of minor league franchises in every sport are historic. As such, they provide an almost pure example for why every business needs to work from a formal strategic plan. If well researched and properly put together, the planning process will reveal who is in the market available for the company to serve, and how best they can be reached. The planning process should lead a company to understand why consumers, particularly the ones that are qualified to be their customers, do not do business with them.

Like the coach putting in the late hours to make sure he's as prepared as possible to win games, every business manager should defend their company with the same work ethic. It takes a deep competitive spirit. It takes a strong will to win and a burning refusal to lose. It requires being honest with your weaknesses and a vigilant attention to competitive threats. Taking market share is a systematic and planned process that can only be as good as the information used for planning. What you think you know makes you vulnerable in a dynamic market.

Success in any competition requires having the right people to execute the plans. A coach knows that there's no substitute for a natural gift. Given the right direction and a solid game system, the excellent athlete will be productive. An awkward or physically inferior player will produce less success. In the same way, marketing processes and systems are simply the steps to prepare for an intellectual evaluation of the conditions of a market and for formulating the steps to take to improve one's position within them. This is always deeply influenced by the level of intelligence of the people making and executing the plans. An IQ of 135 will be more effective in executing the science and art of marketing than an IQ of 100 in the same way a running back that runs a 4.5 second forty-yard sprint will be more valuable than a player with a 5.0 time. Intelligence has a direct impact on the ability to read market indicators and one's adeptness in seeing how all the factors influence each other. It's a smart manager that hires smarter employees, much in the same way the smartest coach will try to find the best players.

When we look at the Steelheads, the marketing focus through their initial years didn't take anything for granted. They weren't selling ice hockey. They were competing for the community's entertainment dollar. They linked their image to the community. They understood that if dollars are invested for promotions to grow attendance with non-fans, they need to be carefully directed to answer four fundamental questions. What is the message that will reach those that have little history with or have had no interest in the product as it has been typically positioned? What will change their habits? Can this message be successful with the budget available? How will success be measured?

There is no single answer to these questions to satisfy all markets. Clearly, with continued declines, the solution to building committed fans for minor league hockey is generally not found in $2.00 beer nights, cheerleaders, between period dodge-ball-on-ice contests, and free parking. The solution is found in a consumer marketing strategy. It begins from knowing what you need to be in order to attract enough support to sustain you. It also should include processes that ensure accountability, including bottom-up management-by-objective incentives and evaluation tools that measure results in the same way athletes are exposed or rewarded through the team's cumulative box scores.

As you look at your business and its day-to-day competitive habits, are they more like the team's business office or coach's office? What don't you know about your competitor? What don't you know about yourself? What are the weaknesses in your staff that need correcting, replacement, or fortification? What can you expect with certainty from your market opponent and what will you do to counter it? How can you win week after week, year after year? For your business, these may not even be the right questions. The answers may not be easy.

The day-to-day management and long-range planning of a business should ensure that each activity meets the tests for winning customers. That is the sole purpose for every action and investment of a company. It is also why it is wise to observe and adopt the habits found within all competitive sports teams. They can teach us the habits that will win marketshare.

In the business section of the book store there are numerous offerings that discuss "How to be Successful" written by coaches that never actually ran a business. They write about the practices that set them above the rest. One needn't visit too many offices in business before running into a Leroy Neiman picture of Vince Lombardi or Bear Bryant with a quote that inspires. How would Vince run your business? How would you answer to Bear Bryant if he wanted to see your plan for winning? Do you approach your business with the competitive preparation and planning that these winners took to their jobs? Every business needs to be guided by people who think like a coach, digging deep to get the knowledge to build a successful plan. Every company needs someone to study the field, know the opponents, and make sure every action supports reaching the company's strategic goals. It's a simple proven fact that winning anything is virtually impossible without preparing for the contest.

GETTING THE RIGHT MIX

Until now, this book has emphasized the value of applying strategic thinking to your planning. It has offered examples of the strategic planning process executed brilliantly. It has shown cases where a short-term focus without considering the long-term dynamics of the business environment has ruined a company. Now it's time to roll up our sleeves and get to the heart of how strategic planning is done. It begins by understanding "The Marketing Mix."

"Marketing Mix" is a term used since the 1940's to discuss the specific elements that can influence the delivery of goods and services successfully to a consumer. These elements have often been referred to as "The Four P's" - Product, Place, Price, and Promotion. As these elements are discussed, you will understand how intertwined they become in practice and how they need to be balanced with each other to ensure the success of a product, service, brand, or company's stability. The well managed marketing mix of a product or service ensures that the features setting it apart are appealing enough to generate ample revenue at the price needed to sustain it through the product life cycle. It includes the most efficient promotional component to maximize the revenue and profit potential.

A Balanced Mix

Ford Motor Company is a monster that needs to constantly be fed by the market. Ford must sell a lot of goods to make a profit. To address this need of the company, they offer a wide range of cars, trucks, and farm equipment built in a variety of factories. Ford's purpose is to sell products designed for the masses. Their product must be priced to appeal to the widest range of purchasers. The products must be competitively featured, dependable and safe, and assembled with a consistent standard of quality. Their existence from model-year to model-year depends on their ability to provide a competitive value that attracts millions of customers to their expansive network of retailers. They combine a broad mix of national media advertising, consumer incentives, retailer support programs, and customer retention campaigns.

Ford makes every effort to present their transportation values to as many automobile and truck customers as possible. So does Chevrolet, Dodge, Toyota, Nissan, Honda, Mazda, Volkswagen, Saturn, Hyundai, Mitsubishi, Kia, Suzuki, and any other company that needs to carve a piece of the available sales from the market in order to keep their company healthy. It's crowded, brutally competitive, and only those capable of delivering the most appealing answer to the needs of consumers prevail.

Rolls Royce, on the other hand, is a product that draws consumers through its reputation. They are made one at a time for the narrowest consumer profile imaginable. Each car is a handcrafted masterpiece ensuring the ultimate in detail and quality. They are works of art. Each product has the latest features, performance, and technology available. The amenities are custom crafted to suit the owner. A Rolls Royce carries a price tag that few others could justify. The price it bears is justified by not only the perfection in fit and finish, the advanced features, and unmatched comfort it delivers, but also its exclusivity. It has almost no competition for its customers. Like Ford, it is a car. But its marketing mix has little in common with Ford's.

Place

The marketing mix begins by understanding comprehensively the "Place" where the product and/or service is to be sold. Who are the competitors and how are they changing? What products do they offer and how does what you offer compare? What customers do you have today that are at risk, and how can their needs be best met to retain them? Are there any product gaps that your company can fill? Understanding the marketplace comes from answering limitless questions that could help position your enterprise with an advantage.

The questions should never be restricted to the competitive pressures of the enterprise. You shouldn't overlook the conditions you can't control within the environment where your products must survive. Have the laws changed? If I'm selling cigarettes or operating a nightclub, what impact does the trend to control secondhand smoke have on my business? If I am a wholesale distribution company, what are the best shipping logistics to serve the customers I need to reach? Are my customers changing their habits because of the convenience of the internet or the increasing cost of shipping? Do these changes expand my market and provide a wider range of prospects?

Having a complete understanding of the marketplace is fundamental to being successful in selling any service or product. If the competitive conditions, economic realities, and best practices within the industry are not understood, a company will not be able to adequately compete and sustain success. Any one of these influences is capable of stopping a product dead in its tracks if overlooked or wrongly assumed. Some unaddressed changes in the market's conditions could bring an enterprise to its end.

Where you do business is fundamental to the kinds of products you will be able to sell. One could sell bottled water via direct mail, but not gasoline. It would be inappropriate to sell fine wines from the Girl Scout Cookie Catalog. Radio Shack would not be the place folks would stop to buy baked goods. A John Deere retailer in Fort Dodge, Iowa probably wouldn't have much additional product turnover if he added Ferrari's. All of these are obvious.

Knowing what happens in the marketplace is critical in knowing how to position your goods and services within it. Identifying the benefits that your competition brings to their customers, and knowing why their customers don't do business with you, is very important. Knowing as much as possible about their customers improves your ability to compete. Understand the features, benefits, pricing, distribution, and promotion methods of your competition. Gain knowledge about their culture and mission. What are the policies and programs that are most attractive to their consumers? Knowing this information can guide the honing of your own practices so that you will deliver unique benefits to the market that give your company an advantage. A company needs to know who they are to the consumer before they begin selling anything. Honestly seeing the company that you work for can be a challenge in itself. Too often the internal "spin" (cheerleading) clouds any understanding of what the company really means to the market.

Product

Understanding the marketplace, the competitors, and its consumers helps guide the engineering and development of goods and services. Product development must be market-focused, developed with a measurable number of prospects, and positioned to evoke a buying decision. Goods must provide obvious benefits that can easily be communicated to the consumer. They must provide unique qualities that distinguish them from the crowd.

An automobile manufacturer is not just selling a machine. They really aren't simply selling solutions to someone's transportation needs, either. The purchase of an automobile is tied to fashion, status, recreation, and a host of other needs and wants of a customer. A hockey game is not just a contest between two teams. It's the way a family can spend time together. It's the way a business person can entertain a client. It's an escape from the daily stresses of life. A pair of $200 blue jeans will make perfect sense to a specific customer profile, but not to the consumer looking for the best deal on a pair of Wranglers.

Suppose a consumer visits two different financial institutions to discuss their investment needs. One lays out an array of products and describes their interest rates, growth expectations, and highlights the specifications of each option. The other skips the data and builds the discussion around the consumer's goals. What kind of education do you want to provide for your daughter? When do you intend to retire? Vacations and recreational purchases are talked about. The consumer isn't buying a financial product that is expected to grow at 5% per annum. They're saving for their daughter's wedding and retiring to a gated resort community under the sun.

Every product a company sells must occupy a sound strategic position that serves the goals of the company. The products that a company sells must meet a definable value-proposition that offers unique competitive advantages against the competitors in the marketplace. Because you can make a two-color facsimile machine doesn't mean you can market one. There must be a welcoming gap in the marketplace with an available avenue that will deliver the goods to the ultimate consumer.

Products must evolve ahead of a pace set by the dynamics of the market. The advent of motorized vehicles required Studebaker to abandon covered wagons and adapt to the wants of automobile consumers. Typewriters were replaced by personal computers so Brother needed to find other opportunities. The new generation of goods and services developed by a successful company must fit their strengths and capabilities as they adapt to the changing conditions of the market.

Some companies are expected to lead and innovate, providing state-of-the-art products that consumers will pay a premium to own. Some are expected to appeal to a budget minded-consumer. The position a brand holds in the marketplace defines its promise to the consumers and the products they will accept. To confuse a brand by introducing elements that are out-of-kilter with the brand's identity is a bad idea. A Packard is not built from Studebaker engines and body panels, and a Ford Taurus frame will never create a Jaguar.

Pricing

The "Pricing" aspect of the marketing Mix has rules. Never be the pricing leader unless your product is inferior. (Inferior doesn't mean poor quality in this context. A Chevy is inferior to a Rolls Royce and it should be reflected in the price). Never price for "loss leadership" unless you are the market leader (or on the verifiable verge of leadership) and eliminating competitive pressure through the cannibalization of the market. Some think that the easiest way to grab a position in the market is to be cheap. It doesn't always work. If it does, it could only be temporary because someone else can always be cheaper. Pricing is a dangerous promotional tool and using lower prices is a highly vulnerable way of growing a business.

If you adopt a pricing philosophy that defends the profits of the company, it will prompt you to be more innovative in your thinking and set the groundwork for stability and survival. The most critical strategy for pricing is to never use it in a way that will not add positive results to your financial picture and contribute to your ultimate long-range strategic goals.

Price discounts do not work unless they produce net gains. If the price is reduced 10%, how many more units must be sold and what will it cost to sell them to produce a positive bottom line result? Always be sure your price will pay for the promotions and sales incentives that were invested to sell it. All advertising and promotion must be justified by the sales they generate and the bottom-line profit picture.

Never use discounted pricing when it isn't needed to meet your goals. Discounting is used best as a guerilla tactic to solve specific and individual competitive pressures. Sometimes it can be carefully used to address specific cash flow needs. Like a surgeon, only cut where necessary and try to minimize the scar. Always be in a position to measure your results.

The person that encourages discounting without a projected outcome for their pricing strategy (detailing specific goals and a defined way to measure them) should be fired. That person threatens the stability of the company and negatively redefines the company in the market. Price can redefine consumer habits when it is reduced with no cause or foresight. When Lee Iacocca used rebates to sell cars, he saved his company. It was purposeful and calculated to produce a needed result based on the consumer's reluctance to visit a Chrysler dealer. Yet, he also created a customer base that does not buy cars without a rebate. At the time this was an acceptable (and even necessary) risk that was justified by the position of the company within the market.

Pricing is a way of communicating to your consumer. It tells them how much you value your products and services. Pricing can serve to underscore a product's image. The Mercedes dealer doesn't typically involve discounting as a means of promoting sales of its exclusive automobiles while the more proletariat consumer drawn to the local Chevy dealer can't escape the campaigns promising "factory invoice pricing." Pricing must speak to the market it is attempting to engage.

The price of a product or service can only support the positive image of a brand when the product outperforms the consumer's expectation. If a product is sold as a lawn mower, it must cut grass. If it is sold as a DVD player, it must perform the functions that DVD player performs. A birthday gift that fails on the day it is unwrapped is a bad product at any price. The price of it makes no difference. "What did you expect for the price?" is not a consumer-focused customer service statement.

Pricing should be built from two directions. The starting point in establishing the price of the product is to establish the fixed and variable costs for running the business. For a minor league hockey team the leases, payroll, utilities, postage, effective advertising should all be addressed in the strategic goals of the plan and reflected in the determination of the pricing. This shouldn't be the only basis for pricing.

The target price should always be determined by what the market will bear. A price that is low may generate more unit sales and a price that is high may reduce unit sales – but knowing whether or not the decision to raise or lower a price benefits the company can only be determined by the need to do so, and measured in specific benefits to the company through marketshare gains, improved cash flow, a reduction in inventory overstocks, and ultimately the bottom-line profits. Unless the price is reduced to address a very specific problem, the lowest price allowable must be the point where unit sales are maximized before showing a diminished return to the bottom line. The highest price must be the point where profits are maximized before the economies of scale are lost, and the decision to increase price any further, produces a diminished return to the bottom line. Good market research should lead you to knowing fairly well the correct pricing to maximize profitability, cash flow and inventory turnover.

Promotion

Once the marketplace is understood, the product is designed to meet its needs, and the price is set to ensure a profitable experience, the fourth "P" needs to be mixed into the strategy – "Promotion." To many, the words "promotion" and "marketing" are interchangeable. They are not. In the marketing mix, promotion is just one important element that needs equal consideration and appropriate focus. An omnipotent and expansive advertising budget may not produce more sales if the product, price, and marketplace cannot support it.

Although it isn't my original idea, perhaps the most important element in successful promotion is to realize that there is no such thing as "mass marketing." Although the television is flooded with ads for cereal, soap, and automobiles, each reaches enough prospective consumers with an individual and very personal message that speaks directly to their needs and wants. "Your breath stinks, and unless you use our mouthwash you'll not get your next promotion and you'll have no chance in attracting the ideal mate." As I'm cupping my hand over my face to see if anyone will ever kiss me again, the next ad tells me that the dog lying in the corner has bad breath, too. Then they then tell me I need to kill the smells in my refrigerator with a box of baking soda. It's all very personal.

When the critical mass of qualified prospects is too great for a personal contact, mass communication tools that can deliver a message that speaks to the personal needs or wants of specifically targeted consumers is the practical answer. If your market size is smaller and the goals of your plan can be achieved through more economical means, mass advertising is wasted. Sometimes a balance between the different methods pays best – mass media campaigns to support the activities of the salesperson on the pavement. The point is, you need to know or you'll be wasting money. Money is the lifeblood of your company. In short, your promotions must make the most of the investment to make them work. It must produce expected and very specific results.

In a nutshell, the "promotion" component of the marketing mix is how you reach your prospects with the benefit message that changes or creates a buying decision. A strategic promotion plan must identify the prospective customers, segment them into "levels of readiness," and estimate the value of reaching each segment. A campaign must make financial sense and include hard tests to measure success. By tracking promotion expenditures against anticipated results, you can discover ways to reshape your message and hone it to produce more effective returns. Promotion should always serve your budget goals and add value to your company.

All Mixed Up

When all the pieces of the marketing mix are in balance, the customers you have identified and targeted are attracted to buy your products with the most efficient promotional expenditure. People will buy when you offer an appealing value-proposition that meets their needs and wants. If your product falls short of the consumer's expectation for performance, it won't sustain sales regardless of the price, promotion, or whatever else is happening in the marketplace. No packaging, no incentive, no slick talking sales message can satisfy a consumer need or want. The marketing mix must be able to adapt and endure through changing conditions in a market. It must anticipate vulnerability and preempt threats. Anticipating the threats that make you vulnerable can be extremely challenging.

Threats can come from out of the blue and strike in ways that you may not be able to imagine. Some emerge from changing conditions you can't control. It isn't our nature to be defending ourselves during the good times. To be asking "what if" can make one sound slightly paranoid during periods of prosperity. But you never can let yourself feel too comfortable. This is why successful company leadership and smart marketing requires bright and flexible individuals that can see themselves from a range of angles.

Gulfstream is an aircraft manufacturer whose customers have typically waited long periods for the delivery of their largest executive jets. The first several years of production for their anticipated G-650 are committed to customers (who have placed millions in deposits to reserve a place in the production plan) long before the jet's scheduled roll-out. The same was true for the G-V and G-550 and several other models that preceded them.

The G-650 will be delivered to its customers for a price in the neighborhood of $60 million. The main customers are not rock stars and Hollywood movie moguls. They are Fortune 500 companies and leading international corporations that manage in-house flight departments with maintenance personnel and flight crews. To the average citizen, this seems obscenely expensive. Yet, the product's price is well within a justifiable threshold when compared against the value it brings to the company.

In terms of marketing mix, Gulfstream sells a jet that has a global range and every imaginable advancement and comfort. For decades, they have steadily built a solid position of leadership from a fertile corporate aviation market. Their product's popularity forced them to establish rules in their buying agreements that ensure profit-takers don't take delivery and then sell the jet for millions more than the factory price (or even sell their place in line before delivery is made). There was big money that could be made as a third-party seller just by having new or newer-used Gulfstream jets available for the purchase-ready market.

When Gulfstream promotes their aircraft, they have a very targeted and efficient message that gets directly to the decision-making prospects that highlights the unique benefits they offer against the competitors. One of the problems, however, is that the manufacturers and the trade organization in the private aviation industry haven't done an adequate job of completely defining the customer that needs selling, *nor* focused on the actual benefits of the product that meet that customer's needs and wants.

It's hard for the lunch-pail gang to see a corporate jet as something more than a perk for the company's executives. But a white paper study revealed that when similar Standard and Poor's 500 companies are compared, the profits of companies that have a private jet solution for executive travel show almost 100% more financial productivity than companies that don't fly private jets. The facts clearly demonstrate that corporations flying their own jets make more money. Additionally, *Time* reported that a Gulfstream G-V bought in 2006 could sell a year later for a price that would generate an $8 million profit for the company. Historically, there has been an ownership cycle that allows a company to buy private jets, fly private jets, and after a few years trade-up their private jets that often results in executives and top-producing employees flying virtually for free.

The earnings improvement that is derived by flying your key personnel on privately-owned and managed jets comes from making your top producing employees more productive. Imagine the typical commercial flight ritual. You wake before the crack of dawn, drive through traffic to a distant airport like Newark, O'Hare, or DFW, shuttle yourself from the parking lot to the check-in counter, stand in line to check in, stand in line to get frisked by security, wait 30 minutes for the flight, fly to your first connection, wait for the flight, fly to the commercial airport nearest your destination, wait for your bags, and then travel to some distant location to do your business. It's a classic, "The early bird gets the worm," story. Regardless of how early you rise, the chances are, if you are flying a commercial jet to do your business, the 'worm" was already gotten by the prudent competitor that was on his way to get his third worm before you even collected your bags.

What makes private aviation the best solution for many major company's top executives and revenue producers is that they can pull up to the hangar of the most convenient airport, walk straight to the plane with their bags, and fly directly to their destination with such efficiency that they can attend four or five meetings in four or five cities every day. While in the air, they can use the fax, phone, and internet connection in the privacy of the cabin. They can continue to conduct their business with security and confidentiality. For highly visible corporate executives who make prime targets for evil-doers, the private aviation solution reduces the risk of kidnapping, hostage taking, or terrorism. The price to take additional staff members is virtually zero.

The product that Gulfstream, Bombardier, Hawker-Beech, and Cessna deliver to their primary customers is improved financial productivity. They eliminate wasted time and they increase the opportunity to produce revenue—which in turn produces a higher EBITDA, greater asset efficiency, and improved returns. In fact, a study revealed that the private aviation business has been typically been driven by the Chief Financial Officers of major corporations. If the case can be made for a company to save money and raise its earnings through a private aviation solution, the chief protector of the company's bottom-line willingly approves the purchase. When the CFO factors in the tax benefits and creative financing available, putting the top revenue producers on a jet is a "no brainer." For years, private aviation has been mysterious to the average citizen. They see jets. They see price tags. They see luxury. They don't see the low monthly installments of the seven-year balloon financing for a workhorse and revenue-building tool that sells seven years later for millions more than its original purchase price.

Since I've mentioned them earlier, if the CEO's of Ford and GM flew a typical commercial airline to Washington, DC, the total time to the airport, the time to make the flight, the time to arrange for transportation, and the inconveniences of check-ins, security screenings, and delayed flight could have cost their company over $100 thousand in measurable lost productivity. It's unlikely that they would make this important trip without advisors and assistants, so add the productivity of the staff members from the legal and accounting departments that might have joined them on top of that expense. The cabin of a "heavy" jet (like those manufactured by Gulfstream) provides all of the amenities an executive needs in order to be as productive as a day at the office.

Depending upon the aircraft chosen, a trip from Detroit to Washington, DC might cost the company as little as $10 thousand and not much more than $25 thousand dollars Flying in the epitome of luxury and comfort, on such a trip GM and Ford most likely saved their shareholders an average of $80,000 each by using the jets they own.

With so many measurable benefits, it is a wonder that the use of private jets has become so negatively perceived by the public. Yet, the marketing mix for the industry never anticipated that public's opinion could ever be a key vulnerability. They weren't prepared for a reckless Congress and news media taking the automobile and financial industries to task for what they perceived to be a thoughtless abuse of trust. It seemed frivolous to the lawmakers in Washington that the chief executives of the car companies could jump on a private jet and wing their way to DC to beg for money. The news media echoed the indignation of these Congressional attacks without the slightest bit of research to understand why so many companies would maintain a jet fleet. But the reality is, motoring in a hybrid automobile from Detroit to DC cost the auto companies more money and created an increased risk of death and kidnapping.

Since the first Learjet 23 darted through the sky in 1963, the private aviation industry has been a huge success. Year after year, new jets and new customers converged in an industry that over the last decade grew at a rate exceeding 20% each year. As I listened to the sales director of a manufacturer talk about his company's strength, size, product line, back order situation, and international expansion and presence, there wasn't a hint that he could imagine being vulnerable to anything. Yet, the marketing mix was faulty because the manufacturers failed to position their products for the genuine values they offer to the businesses they support *and* they did not include all of the owners of the companies they sell in the targeting of their promotions. That left them vulnerable to the incompetence of their customers. When the spokesperson at General Motors was asked by a reporter why his Chief Executive flies on a private jet, the response was no different than a kid caught with his hand in the cookie jar. "It's our company's policy," was no answer.

In the case of the private aviation industry, the marketing mix should have understood the responsibility their corporate clients have to the company's shareholders as an always current condition of the market. A key factor of success would be to manage a marketing mix in which the product was "corporate earnings" and the promotion included assurances to shareholders that the jet was a tool for building revenue. Instead of positioning it as a luxury and reward for achieving an elevated position deserving the epitome of excess, it might have been positioned so we'd accept them as a reality of a well-run company much the way we view a farmer needing a $300 thousand tractor. The farmer could plant his crops with a $19 hoe, but the time it would take to farm that way would not let him plant as much, as quickly. In the same way, the top producer for a major corporation can plant more seeds and harvest more results if provided the right tools.

The lesson to be learned from the private aviation industry's problem is that regardless of how well things are going, potential vulnerabilities must be vigilantly pursued with systematic solutions. When things are going well, it's hard to see vulnerabilities. In this case, forgetting that the company's shareholders are actually the people that own the jet created an error in defining the product in a way that the owners would embrace. The media's perception of the corporate jet revealed a gap in how the products, the companies, and the industry as a whole are promoted. Throughout the marketing mix there was an unbalanced focus on the nuts and bolts of the product and the high price of ownership, and far too little on the values they produce for the owners.

This is an important point for all businesses. The marketing mix of any product or service must be balanced to ensure its survival through any impending threat as long as the product is valid. Threats are not always obvious. There is always something you aren't expecting lurking to bring you harm.

MOST ADVERTISING IS A WASTE

I had a young salesman in Louisiana in the early 1980's who was a huge fan of the weekly football gambling pool. When I joined him in a hotel restaurant for breakfast one morning, he had the form on which he'd mark his favorite teams on the table, and a "tip sheet" in his other hand. I said "good morning," grabbed a menu, and left him to evaluate his choices while I selected what I was going to eat.

It was a pretty interesting process to watch over the top of the menu. He took this weekly ritual much more seriously than the schedule of work we had ahead of us. (Of course, I was in The South, and in The South there's not much that is more important than God, Country, and football. In fact, if you stay long enough, you'll realize that for many they may even all be the same thing.)

After I ordered, I asked him, "Kelly, does that tip sheet actually make you any money?"

He said it really didn't, "But my uncle makes a ton of money from it."

"Your uncle gambles on football?" I asked.

"No," he answered. "He's the guy who publishes the tip sheet."

This conversation has always influenced my understanding of the relationship between the money I spend on advertising and the people who accept it. The tip sheet cost a dollar. His uncle sold a few thousand of them every week. Like Kelly, it isn't likely that everyone buying one was seeing a lot of benefit from the dollar they spent. Still, it was great business for the uncle. The reason this made an impression on me is that it gives a pretty good example of the kind of relationship many companies have with their advertising agencies.

Any book about marketing must discuss advertising. Discussing advertising must be in the context of the promotional element of the marketing mix. But it also must recognize that advertising agencies, the commercial media, and the presses that print collateral sales materials, represent industries that thrive on generating revenue from their clients. As such, their conversations with you are framed in human motivations, personal needs, and quiet ambitions that may not always align themselves with your needs and concerns. What they do for you will always appeal to your ego. This is the fun part of the marketing job – creative, artful, and personally fulfilling. Yet, unless objectively and carefully managed, most of what these entities do for you won't directly add a nickel to your bottom-line objectives.

In order to start talking about advertising, let's take it down to its basic elements. To sell a rusted 1953 Chevy, the promotion could be as simple as writing "For Sale" on a piece of paper, sticking the piece of paper in the car's window, and parking the car on the side of the road. Viewed strategically, setting the car at the side of a well-traveled parkway gives it the most affordable exposure to the highest number of qualified prospects. The targeted market understands the particular vehicle's ability to satisfy their individual needs. The production expense maximizes the probable return. Deciding which roadway and the size of the sign are key factors that influence the results. Would you get more attention by running a series of radio ads or buying the billboard under which you pushed the car? Probably. But it wouldn't make any sense.

The methods for promoting a company, a brand, a product, or a service, include the salespeople and sales support personnel, advertising in newspapers, television, radio, internet, street teams with flyers or samples, in-store demonstrations, and billboards. Direct mail, websites, and catalogs can be effective means for making sales. The signage on buildings and vehicles create a repeatedly seen image of a company that creates brand awareness. Community sponsorships like the Little League or the Boy and Girl Scout units create positive exposure. The choices are unlimited. Because there are so many options, every choice must meet the test of serving the company's overall strategy by focusing on a specific, measurable goal.

The goal of promotion is to reach the maximum number of well-qualified prospects, with the least investment, in order to produce the biggest improvement toward the strategic objectives of the company. A young dentist I knew took a long-term strategy that reached into specific segments of the community and got him involved with prospective patients. He offered free custom-made mouth-guards for a local youth hockey team. The mothers of the kids would jump on an offer like that. His thinking, which actually worked, was that by the time the fitting was over, the kid and his mom would often decide that they needed to become regular patients of this new dentist. The young dentist was cultivating younger patients that would ensure his future. He used a strategy that eventually might actually result in him looking after the oral health of the children of these first patients.

The Good Humor Man attracts his business by painting pictures of ice cream bars on his truck and announcing himself in the neighborhood with a familiar song. He wouldn't be wise to invest in a radio campaign, take out a yellow page ad, or send a press release to the local paper to increase business. Instead, he might find the communities with a high concentration of kids, turn the loudspeaker a little higher, and drive a little slower. He might schedule his route so he arrives at the community pool just as swim lessons are ending. There he would find beamingly proud parents with treat-loving children begging to be served.

Every promotion should be as perfect as the Good Humor Man's. The promotion should identify the targeted segment and the segment size must justify the cost. If you manufacture products to be sold through the office specialty retailer, you'll need a strong salesperson who understands the paradigms for success in this channel of business. You'll supply him or her with detailed catalogs, adequate point-of-sale materials, product service centers, and an attractive budget (justified by the retailer's commitment) to support the retailer's advertising schedule and merchandising needs. You wouldn't need a full-blown television ad campaign or a weekly exposure in *Newsweek.*

Promotional expenses should produce measurable results. If you wanted to boost sales in the home office product category, a radio advertising campaign may not produce justifiable results. It may not fit the business' needs. It may waste budget by reaching every non-prospect that hears the radio campaign at the same cost that could have reached more qualified prospects through another method. Dollars allocated for promotion without a manner for measuring return, are spent recklessly. Additionally, the value of a well-done campaign increases if it does not restrict itself to influencing a single buying decision. The ultimate goal should be to re-program a consumer buying habit.

Any promotion must match how the goods are purchased. This is vital to success, yet there are classic examples where this is overlooked. In the late 1970's, Schlitz beer was a top-three brand. While their fall from this stature can be traced to a range of conditions, among them was an advertising campaign that showed a rugged lumberjack sitting on a log and virtually challenging the manhood of anyone that would drink something else. I recall my own reaction the first time I saw it – it left my jaw agape. If it had been a Saturday Night Live joke, it would still have been in bad taste.

The campaign was clearly designed to appeal to the "macho" characteristics of its male consumers and seemed not to be a bad idea considering the majority of beer consumers during this period of time were male. It was a brash "in-your-face" campaign with a product message that was intended to appeal to the egos of flannel shirted he-men. The Schlitz message was simple - if you want to be a masculine man, you need to drink this masculine and manly Schlitz beer.

If the ad was surprising to me, it most surely was offensive to women (especially during the emergence of a Gloria Steinem-influenced women's movement). More importantly, it failed to consider the one key reality of beer marketing. They overlooked the need to appeal to the significant number of women that went to the store to make the beer purchase on behalf of their husbands. Women in the 1970's were the ones buying the groceries. The people who made beer purchases, the women, didn't want that kind of man anywhere near their homes.

Television, radio, and billboards are generally unavoidable mediums for getting a company, brand, product or service in front of consumers in an intrusive and unavoidable way. Internet pop-ups and direct mail may also fall in these categories. The PowerBall billboard that announces, for a mere dollar, you have a chance to win $200 million is likely to steer more than a few cars to the local mini-mart.

Non-intrusive ads generally support consumers that are looking to be served. Magazine and newspaper advertising can be both intrusive and non-intrusive. Grocery store coupons, cinema display ads, and tire retailer promotions appear in newspapers with predictable schedules that reach consumers when their buying state is highest. Their resource value is that they develop steady and supportable buying patterns in a class of consumers. Yellow Pages, websites, and industry directories are non-intrusive and reach the consumers specifically when they are prepared to buy. As the tow truck is pulling your Taurus station wagon off the side of the road, you'll probably grab the Yellow Pages to select the transmission repair shop where your car will be dropped.

The best medium to use for your promotion can be determined by dividing the cost by the number of qualified impressions it delivers. An "impression" is simply one prospect seeing your message. The newspaper's circulation, the number of people in the cars that pass the billboard, the viewers of the evening news, and the number of ears listening to the radio station that hear your message represent impressions. The number of qualified prospects that are exposed to your message determines the value you will get for your promotional effort.

The mistake many make is to spend their budgets for as many impressions as possible without testing the quality of each impression. Knowing the current conditions of your market allows you to balance your campaign with media that systematically reaches the largest servable segment of qualified prospects from the bigger market. A budget will go further to improve the health of an enterprise if it is focused on the most qualified prospects.

Think of it this way. A coyote is no match for a herd of steer, but he does have a tactic for separating his dinner from it. Identify the promotional medium that reaches the greatest number of quality prospects in your targeted segment, and you will be supporting your sales goals economically. Select the method that is capable of delivering your message to an audience with the highest "buying state," and if your product matches their needs, you will produce the best possible result. Hit them with an ad directly on their common decision factors (don't mix your message), you will create customers.

To ensure that your promotions will work, you must instantly respond to the customer's orders. It sounds very simple, but there are businesses that will concentrate on the first few points without adequately addressing the final point. They will run promotions without the ability to support it successfully with inventory or manpower. They will run ads to produce more business without a thought for how much business they should raise to make sense of the expenditure. If you spend x-number-of-dollars on a campaign, it should deliver a predictable response. That response should be supported with the goods or services being promoted ready to be delivered swiftly and within the consumer's expectations. Long before the ad delivers the predictable result, you need to ask, "Have I prepared to reap the revenue?" A company advertising to a targeted segment, but not prepared to service the responses to the ad, is wasting valuable promotional dollars and creating more ill-will than good.

A strong advertising campaign understands that it is not the product, rather the benefits of the product, that appeal to the consumer. Why would a mom want to bring her family to an ice hockey game? What message would make a business man drive to an arena instead of a restaurant in order to entertain clients? What medium will best reach them? What promotions will attract them? What incentives will secure them? All ads should sell the benefits of a product or service as they appeal to the consumer. Instead of ads that say, "Buy a ticket," they should say, "Buy this smile!" or "Secure this new customer." Let's show a mom a wholesome place where she can taker her 12-year-old boy. Show her where "high-fives" and hugs are part of the joy.

Non-performing ads are found in every industry. Too often, the advertising agency's creative development is directed without the objectivity necessary to understand the consumer's motivation. The used car dealer that puts his cute four-year-old daughter on TV to stutter through some brand promise is not likely to appeal to the audience in a way that will spark a buying decision. Think of how often you've walked into someone's office and said, "Do you have some time to show me pictures of your kids? How about pets? Got any great pictures of your cat?" How does a "Buy from my dad" message appeal to the purchasing "hot button" of the audience it is presented to? How could it be expected to sell product?

If advertising is launched without specific expectations, its value is impossible to track. Without specifically defined expectations, the advertising may fail to address the core needs or wants of the targeted consumer with a message that stimulates a purchase. If the decision about the design and copy of an ad is based on personal, internal feel-good intangibles (and not on setting specific measurable goals with quantifiable results), it is irresponsible and wasteful.

A General Manager of a minor league hockey team boasted to me about his award-winning ad campaign, even while his attendance spiraled downward. His disconnection from what his agency was supposed to be doing for him was astounding. The advertising agency continued to send him invoices for ads that did not bring customers, and by paying for the results produced, the General Manager was failing to protect his company. A trophy stood in the lobby of a company where I once worked that represented a costly campaign that didn't generate one new customer. I've managed two promotional campaigns that were awarded industry recognition, yet failed to produce even one-third of the expected results.

Believing that advertising will work because it is designed by an "award winning" agency is like a hockey coach saying, "We've got the best goalie because he always draws the highest bid in the bachelor charity auction." Looking good is hardly enough. Effective ads include a benefit message to motivate the consumer to buy. Ads should answer their targeted customer's fundamental question, "What's in it for me?" When the ad agency presents their work to a marketing director, specific questions must be answered before committing a nickel to a campaign. Who will it sell? How big is that market? How much is that market worth? How much revenue will it produce? How much will it cost per new customer cultivated? Why will it work? How will you know? Of course these test questions should be applied to all promotional expenditures in all industries (not to exclude the wages, benefits, and incentives provided to the personalities within the sales organization).

These questions are just a start. If you were buying a new copier for the office, it's very likely that you'd compare machines based on the basic cost of the machine and the cost-per-copy based on supplies and maintenance. Advertising should be held to the same scrutiny. If it doesn't work to make money in a measurable way, it is probably costing money and not effective in meeting the strategic goals of the company. Suppose you had a salesperson on the payroll that didn't produce a new customer or sales increase in five years. Would you keep paying him? I have worked with eight different advertising agencies in my career. Only one made me money. Because of this, I would suggest that every company establish specific expectations for their advertising and restructure their agency relationship so that the agency shares accountability. In very broad terms, advertising as it is practiced by many advertising agencies is a creative process devoid of responsibility for the outcome.

To many agencies, ads are more about art than business. It's a product they sell that features clever graphics and catchy copy. If it works (and sometimes it does), the creative and production is billed at a rate of hundreds-of-dollars per hour, and the media buy generally has a commission tacked on to it. When an advertisement fails, it still gets billed at the same lofty cost. The hockey GM mentioned before may have won a local Cleo, but the team lost nearly 1/3 of its published attendance during the years they paid the agency's retainer.

The campaigns developed by advertising agencies frequently have more to do with politics and the "schmooze" between the account executive and the company's leadership, than tangible and targeted strategic marketing. At $175 per hour, one agency principal explained to me that, "Our success is directly a result of the direction we receive." One problem in managing advertising agencies is that many people that engage their services do not have the training to evaluate their proposals, or experience to test for a predictable result. They get "wowed" by the colors and catchy slogans without knowing who, other than those in the company, will buy products from the message that is being broadcast.

Because so few who in a company understand the definitive science of marketing, there are times when the person primarily responsible for the success of the advertising runs into roadblocks that prevent its improvement. In my own experience, I joined a company that had over-spent their budget by three times. The money spent produced nothing for the company's bottom line. They had great posters, lots of slick post cards, and a trophy for the display case. When I suggested a different direction the President was blunt. As if coached by the agency, he said, "There are a lot of ways to get where we need to be. These things take time." I pressed him by showing flaws in the campaign that nobody was buying. He replied, "This is the campaign the chairman picked. Do you think you're smarter than him?" Congratulations to the agency. They did the job they need to for the agency.

If the President of this company's question had any validity, one could assume that Jerry Jones' Dallas Cowboys wouldn't need a coach to stand at the sidelines, draw up the plays, and to run the practices for the team. Jerry's richer than any of the viable coaching prospects. He's won more Super Bowls. Based on that alone, we can assume that he certainly he has a better grip on football than anyone that he could hire to do the job. In terms of my conversation with the boss, the conversation was over.

The fundamental problem with the campaign was that it wasn't driven by any real focus on consumer needs that were drawn from a bottom-up understanding of the market. It didn't crystallize any unique customer benefits delivered by the brand. Like the expression of love found in a Hallmark card on Valentine's Day, it defined the value-proposition of the company in boiler-plate, feel-good copy that any company could claim. The President of the company said, "There's a lot of ways to get where we need to be" without actually defining the direction we were heading. That, in short, is the problem with many (but not all) ads. They don't actually take you to someplace advantageous.

For ad agencies to serve efficiently, someone needs to keep them tied to the specific goals of the strategic plan. All but one agency that I have hired avoided specific measurements of results. Almost all of them felt a need to remind me of the statistics regarding the number of impressions it takes before an ad works. If nobody is buying your message, the Account Executive from the agency will regularly recommend that the ad needs more exposure. The agency will suggest that it be run a little longer or given a chance in another medium. Again, they are an independent business depending on you for the revenue that sustains them. They aren't your partner unless they share the risk.

Running a successful campaign requires that you verify and confirm that the audience it will reach matches the campaign's objective. A few years ago I worked to reintroduce a guitar brand that represented the first guitar owned by more 35-year-or-older players than any other. There wasn't much money budgeted to get the product launched, so every available dollar had to be spent for maximum return. As expected, research suggested that the most likely customers would come from the market segment already familiar with the brand. The goal was to create as many impressions as possible with consumers over 35-years-old.

My promotional objectives led me to the two key magazines serving the guitar player – *Guitar World* and *Guitar Player*. *Guitar World's* reach was bigger by far, with a circulation 100% greater than the other. The advertising cost was only 60% greater. In a casual observation, the cost-per-impression suggested the magazine with the bigger circulation cost far less per impression – I'd spend 60% more of my budget to reach 100% more prospects. Yet, what seemed to be a reasonable conclusion, needed to be looked at more closely.

The strategically-minded wouldn't be satisfied by the advertisement's cost-per-impression exposure based strictly on circulation numbers. It was important to know the qualified value of the impressions. Demographics provided by the magazines showed sixty-seven percent of the smaller magazine's readers were over thirty-five, while only two-percent of the bigger magazines readers were that old. Although the bigger magazine reached the most consumers, the smaller magazine reached the greatest number of targeted consumers. In fact, for each dollar spent, the smaller magazine produced 3.7 more targeted prospects. This is a smart exercise to apply to any advertising and promotion strategy. But it is only the beginning. You must pay attention to the results.

Once an advertising campaign begins producing results, the product purchasing consumers can help you to fine-tune the campaign. For example, should the results of a campaign designed primarily to reach a category of over-35-year-old consumers actually produce significant sales from a demographic under that age, the promotion plan may need to be reevaluated. Having specific objectives for every campaign, and evaluating results against those objectives, can be very valuable in keeping your advertising expenditures in check. To know who your promotions draw, their age, sex, ethnicity, and the communities where they live, can provide vital information to tell you if what you are doing is working, indicate markets you may have overlooked, and identify areas where redirecting the promotional expense will bring a stronger return.

This is a strategic approach that continues to evaluate, collect information, and focus based on the successes and failures against the objectives. It is starkly different than a campaign that is launched because, "We've got to keep our name out there in the marketplace." It is impatient with the notion that ads failing to produce measurable results are actually benefiting the company in some way that isn't recorded on the P&L sheet. It keeps a close watch on outgoing expenditures. It remembers that every company is absolutely vulnerable.

Corporate-image ad campaigns are a great way for ad agencies to build their bank account. Most companies should avoid them. The market leaders can justify this kind of campaign in order to grow the market as a responsibility of their leadership position. Large corporations do benefit from strong image pieces to build shareholder confidence. Yet, these are purposeful and integrated into the strategic goals of the company. Every other campaign must be designed with the intent to generate revenue in the predictable fashion of a gumball machine. Put in your coin, get a predictable mouthwatering return.

Geico Insurance has three campaigns that hit us simultaneously. They have a lizard that talks about the value of their product while reinforcing the brand name. They take the mystery out of dealing with an on-line insurance company by using a caveman to remind us how easy it can be. If you ever have a claim, you know they will be quick and supportive in addressing it because of a testimonial campaign that features regular customers with augmented messages from celebrities like Peter Graves and Peter Frampton. All three campaigns have become part of the popular culture. If they tried to pack all of the messages in one single campaign, it wouldn't make much of an impression at all.

It is possible to run a successful campaign that does speak to a wide range of features and values offered by a brand, if it can crystallize the value in a single position-defining message. Wonder Bread, in a crisp and memorable slogan, told mothers that their kids would be healthier in a multitude of ways if they ate the Wonder product. This kind of positioning can be very tricky, however, if all the other elements of the marketing mix are not in place to ensure its success. Advertising campaigns rarely make sales by themselves.

I once armed a sales organization with materials for their presentations that defined over a dozen values of doing business with their company. Each of these selling-points exceeded the standards of the industry, and when combined, delivered a single consumer-value message that neutralized all other competitive threats. We just needed someone that could sell it. I asked the company's Executive Vice President of Sales if he could name the elements of this unique value-proposition off the top of his head. He couldn't. If I gave him a month to study them, he wouldn't. As a result, any campaign that would be launched to promote this message would not produce results because the leadership of the sales organization was comfortable doing business as he had done it for twenty years. He had his sales story and it wasn't going to change.

While stating that advertising should work with the predictability of a gumball machine, there is a caveat. Ads that are designed with urgency driven by offer expirations may evoke an instant response, yet will most often be forgotten once the deadline passes. This is okay for tires and other industries where people are in a high buying state. Put an oil change coupon in the mail, and the discount is likely to drive a reasonable amount of revenue. However, in many situations where you are trying to cultivate a long-term customer relationship, a single ad that is not an integrated component of a larger and thoughtful campaign, does not make the best use of the budget.

It is a mistake to think advertising will create business for you. Instead, as part of a comprehensive formal strategic plan, advertising is one aspect of promotion worth considering. It's best to think comprehensive campaigns. Identify the prospects, find out where they are, crystallize your message, and gain them as a customer. Your promotions are working if they defend your current client base against competitive pressures, or they cultivate a change in enough individual consumers' buying habits to grow your business. If your promotional campaigns produce a bottom-line improvement with a measurable value, you have managed your promotions successfully.

NO FORGIVENESS (FOR WHAT THEY DO NOT KNOW)

A sales-driven company (as opposed to a market-driven company) exists in a culture that looks backwards. It sets goals projected from the company's past history which are massaged into a financial plan to show a profit at the end of the year.

Planning this way is an annual ritual for many companies, large and small. Field salespeople give their territory's sales projections for the next year to their national sales managers. The sales manager then presents his projection to the president, who adds his own spin based upon the owner's, CEO's, or board of director's needs and schedule. By the time the sales goals are worked into the annual budget, they are just a number based on history, and determined by a series of personal agenda. A sales-driven strategy is fuzzy.

Let's take a look at the classic "sales-driven" thinking of the president of a company we will call "Oblique International." He epitomized the kind of decisions that create a very predictable downward spiral in a sales-driven company. Oblique International was a twenty-five-year-old wholesale distribution company before the owner cashed out and sold the company to a financially-driven capital investment firm 3,000 miles away.

When the new owners selected the person they were convinced was an experienced and capable leader to guide their investment, they also weren't sure if he was a qualified "CEO" candidate. So they installed him as the president with a promise not to immediately install anyone else in the top position. They wanted to give him a chance to produce the results they were looking for, and held the position out to him as an incentive. Anxious to impress the board of directors, his staff, and the 130 rank-and-file employees, he was quick to set the company on a new course. On his first day, the new President enthusiastically announced a "new era" for the company in which he would "cut pricing aggressively and grab market share." He wanted to put his own fingerprint on the identity of the company.

In the role as the company's primary leader, he abandoned the written strategic plan of his predecessor, the history and position of the company, and acted swiftly to correct what he believed were the errors that kept the company from reaching its maximum potential. It is worth noting that before he was put in the driver's seat, the company had shown growth and recorded profits in all the previous twenty-five years but one. The company had a history of preserving gross margins, generating fluid cash flow, and only exposed themselves to the most limited accounts-receivable risks.

With the company's market-conquering direction of its new leader, the price slashing strategy was to get the attention of old customers and uncultivated prospects. He was willing to accept the risk of offering liberal credit terms to attract a wider range of retailers. In his "new era," the company used lower prices to cultivate top-tier retailers to uncover limitless new opportunity. Unfortunately, this new positioning was out-of-kilter with the proven marketing mix of the company. It also failed to answer the question, "What about tomorrow?"

Being founded on no more than a hunch, there was no assurance that the new strategy would produce sustainable benefits. There was no plan for measuring results. There was no substantive intelligence to assure him that this rash strategy wouldn't do any more than release inertia that would deeply cut into the company's profit picture. He hadn't any concern that he would be pursuing an aggressive plan to turn them into something they weren't, for a position they didn't have in the minds of their customers, to serve a market with no real motivation to respond.

What made the company unique before he took its control was that they provided an important service that helped smaller, independent retailers survive. The price slashing plan did not fit the capabilities and needs of the company's core of customers or the company's position in the market. For twenty-five years the company's established business model was to serve a significant roster of smaller "mom and pop" enterprises with fair prices, same-day shipping, and COD terms. These retailers depended upon the company's deep inventory and fast shipping in order to keep their cash flow healthy. The "product" Oblique sold them was convenience and dependability. They helped their customers stay in-stock with fresh inventory delivered once or twice a week with replenishment orders that averaged under $300 or less. They offered a fair price, quick delivery, and cash-on-the-barrelhead payment terms that helped the weakest retailer to successfully compete. There would be no reasonable expectation under these conditions that marketshare gains could be won through sweeping price reductions. Absolutely none.

Oblique International drifted away from its established business model. All of the energy was focused on the short-term. The fundamental problem was that the distributor's President was racing against the clock to show strong results for his board. This brought tragic consequences to the company and the employees that had devoted much of their lives to its success. The decision to lower prices to gain market share was monumental in describing how little the President knew about how to make his company successful. Lowering prices to gain market share would not generate more sales from his core customers because their COD orders were limited by their available cash. Instead, profits were shortened which made Oblique less sound. The "new era" launched by the ambitious President was one of failure. It started the inertia that continued after his separation from the company, and ended when the enterprise was acquired by its strongest competitor for little more than a song. Predictably, the investment firm cut their losses and got out.

Without respecting the company's strengths or knowing the customer, and with no deep understanding of the competitor, the most common solution to problems in a sales-driven environment is to reduce price. Unfortunately, thoughtless price-discounting tactics relinquish the value of the products to the retailer, define you to the consumer, and shorten the profits necessary for customer support and new product development. Ultimately, they reduce the value of the company.

A marketing-driven strategy is a far more useful way to plan because it is based on a defined opportunity with measurable and meaningful goals. Its foundation is grounded within the current conditions of the competitive battlefield. It is wrapped in verifiable and tested information. It includes more breadth than a hopeful guess. It tempers a company's progress by filtering ego, politics, and reckless opportunism from every decision. It uses the previous year's results only as a basis for looking introspectively at how things might have been done differently in order to capitalize on the potential of the next year.

Because much of the language for marketing is derived from a military culture, it makes sense to think like a commanding General when engaging in the battles of your marketplace. Before a General commits any significant resources, he is clear on the conditions to expect and the probability for victory. The commander is not going to accept the risks of a battle without being sure that the commitment of resources will help to ensure progress toward a larger objective. A platoon of soldiers is not going to be sent into harm's way on a mission that is based on the idea that "we need to do something."

Furthermore, a field commander is not necessarily going to use the same tactics to secure a bridge as he would to neutralize an enemy communication center. He will begin by knowing the long-term objective, and will be sure that each action supports an ultimate "big picture" goal. He will strategize to be sure every tactic contributes to succeeding in the bigger war. A field commander starts with an assessment of what his men will be facing, so he can direct them strategically to promise victory. It is a systematic approach, with human life as the greatest measure of accountability. It begins by seeing opportunity in a rapidly changing situation, having a clear grip on the foe's strengths and weaknesses, recognizing the value of the success against the resources committed to achieve it, and it ensures the resources are available to deliver the projected outcome.

Marketing-driven companies establish a product's value based upon consumer needs and market conditions. They respond to the product's position in the mind of the consumer, choose the most effective way of delivering goods, and systematically gain marketshare against competitive pressure. If price is the best way to defend a company's bottom line, the thorough strategic planning process of the marketing-driven enterprise will dictate such.

The example of Oblique International illustrates common mistakes that are made within sales-driven companies. In this example, linear thinking worked like this: "If I add value to the company, I will be promoted to the CEO position, and I will make more money." The President figured he had about six months for this to work. So, he lowered prices and accepted every deal available in an effort to inject instant top-side results. In physics, Isaac Newton said that there's no action that doesn't create an equal and opposite reaction. Unfortunately, there is no promise that the actions you take when marketing a company will produce Newton's "equal and opposite" positive reaction. Sometimes, the littlest decision can bring limitless success. Sometimes it can set unimaginable devastation in motion.

When a company is sales-driven, it allows itself to be reactive instead of proactive. Decisions are based on trusted experience. In a strategic plan a company's long-term goals are quantified and its strategies are organized to systematically engage in thoughtful battles for revenue. With a deep knowledge of current conditions and key factors for success, the company can always have the advantage in these battles. Thoughtful strategies are justified by their long-term value before they can be supported by financial resources and manpower. When viewed through objective methods for measuring progress and success, many non-productive distractions, knee-jerk reactions, and deadly hunches are easily avoided. When you go to war for marketshare, a well-constructed strategic plan will arm you for success.

The hubris of company leaders that believe they know their business, and have no need to invest the time in long-range planning, will predictably result in a company being unprepared for the kinds of changes that ultimately threaten its survival. Without a plan for the things that can go wrong, they may respond to a crisis by "acting in the moment" with seemingly prudent layoffs, shut downs, selling off assets, or other reactionary steps that can set the momentum for ultimate demise. These are actions of those who surrender to their changing times, and the environments that impede success, without considering the possible need for the company's fundamental reinvention. A long-range planning process can reveal actions a company can execute that protect its well-being and even elevate its position in the competitive order of the marketplace.

It's common for managers of sales-driven entities to operate within a limited time-frame and with internally-focused objectives such as revenue growth, product expansions, and new customer acquisitions. They count on past experiences to be enough preparation for the company to exist in the conditions of the moment. When major changes influence an industry or market, these attributes are not enough by themselves to protect a company. Not now. Not ever.

Oblique International makes a point that should be of interest to venture capital firms and absentee owners that emphasizes the value of a strategic approach to every holding in their portfolio. With a financial focus only, Oblique gave a personal incentive package to the President of the company that eventually sparked a serious reduction in the company's value. Through it all, the President was confident in his assurances to the owners that the company was on course and in good hands. Without a formal plan as the ultimate report card to track the company's activities, the owners had no choice but to rely faithfully in a belief that the person they put in place had some idea that what he was doing would work.

The absentee owners of a company, regardless of their short-term intention, should keep a long-range strategic approach to the oversight of their portfolio companies. When run by people whose incentives are to produce short-range results, they may overlook critical conditions and miss real opportunity in their markets. When there are no stated and written objectives, no significant measurement of progress aside from the financial reports, and only short-term incentives, they create a scenario in which they tempt their leaders to respond with optimistic deceptions. The relationship that Oblique's President had with its owners is pretty common and speaks to a significant issue regarding the management of absentee-owned businesses.

Absentee-owners and venture capitalists that operate largely on sales-driven and bottom-line financial incentives are asking for trouble. I've seen the president of a company report profound growth in some segments of a business that were the result of an accounting department decision that reassigned sales that were already being generated to different line item of the financial reports. I've seen the absentee owner accept the positive news that a company added dozens of new customers, which actually were regained customers that the company managed to not have done business with for two or three years. I've squirmed through meetings in which the owner's were flat-out lied to by the president, with the justification that it was a "white lie," that things would work out, and "with all the owners had to deal with in their other portfolio companies, there was no reason to cause them concern."

In these cases the company's owners were given information to mask the fact that business was bad, that the company had a customer retention problem and the investments to grow revenue were failing. In all three cases a serious threat to the company was presented as a glowing measure of success. To battle against these obfuscations, an owner might consider having incentive programs based on specific objectives established in a strategic plan that cannot be deceptively reported.

A market-driven plan gives shareholders, partners, vested employees, CEO's, and absentee owners a vehicle to discuss pertinent issues in the context of specific goals. With a formal business plan, objectives are established based on real opportunity, and the activities executed to achieve them are well defined to produce a specific and measurable result. A written strategic plan allows for a thoughtful discussion to determine whether or not the specific tactics are working. A conversation that pertains to the actions that had been chosen because of their high probability for success is a more meaningful discussion than, "Why are the revenues so low?" In the first scenario, the conversation that ensues will focus on thoughtful solutions. A plan creates the format for meaningful dialog and constructs the foundation for a measured reaction devoid of accusations and ego. Most other scenarios foster nothing useful.

LEMMINGS TO THE SEA

The working environment installed at Brother by Gunji contrasts deeply with the kinds of businesses where history and experience dictate the next steps. It differs from closed organizations where financial information is tightly held and fear of the boss leads to compliance to anything he or she says. It eclipses environments where poor management decisions are unchallenged by those closest to the issues because of an understood threat of career derailment for disagreeing, or an anticipation of being rewarded for agreeing.

Many business leaders like the sound of their own voices, especially when they are repeated by their underlings. Offering a contrary view in such a culture can get one labeled as "trouble." As a result, like lemmings to the sea, staff members march in lockstep into a bay of faulty knowledge without the smallest voice questioning the wisdom. This creates a dangerous threat from within a company. When constructive dialog is stifled by your political structure, you hurt yourself. Of course, it is important to also remember that Gunji only gave one the opportunity to prove their ideas. If your mouth opened with some idea to change things for the better, you better have had a solid argument.

It isn't unusual for bosses to cultivate a relationship with their staff that is of the "if I want your opinion I'll give it to you" variety. When opinions are asked for in this situation, the staffers give their best guess to know what the boss wants to hear. When the relationship between a leader and his employee is based on intimidation and politics, the result is good money being paid for wages to people that can't be trusted.

Can a company continue to redefine itself to meet the needs of the market when it encourages "Pavlovian" responses from its decision makers? Of course not.

In the Western business culture "Yes Men" are not mythical, they exist everywhere. Job security is presumed to be ensured when you know what the boss wants. Like the ticking metronome that prompted salivation from Pavlov's dog, the "Yes Man" is ready to swallow anything fed to him by the boss. If the boss is right and you agree, you must be right too. If he's smart, you must be smart, too. However, there are times when the boss will be wrong. A challenge every boss faces is to know how to judge the value of their echoed voice.

The man working on the airplane to create a case to move the company where the CEO wanted to live would not have succeeded in the culture Gunji created. When Gunji listened to his sales divisions present their plans, he did so with his mind opened to newly revealed opportunity. He expected detail. He picked the plans apart, looking for holes, gaps, and incomplete answers. He was quite adept and skillful at challenging the unsubstantiated. Presenting the strategies for a product category, or an entire division, could get uncomfortable. But, Gunji never approached the process with his mind made up. He could not afford to manage his ambition for the company without a method for staying ahead of the market dynamics.

For any company to make strides toward its strategic goals, systems should be in place to permit the individuals who are more specialized, closer to the matter at hand, and most immediately influenced by the results, to guide their outcomes. The doors should be open for discussion, innovation, and fresh principles. Thoughtful debate should be welcome. That is the cornerstone of a bottom-up, market-focused management structure. It realizes that the vitality of a company in a dynamic market can't be assured when workers stay low to the ground, doing their jobs with their mouths shut, simply ensuring they will collect a check on Friday.

On the other hand, just because the employees are talking doesn't mean they are right. The things they say deserve to be challenged. "Well, that sounds good – why will it work?" If the next words from their mouth are "I think" or "I feel," be sure to send them to get some real basis for their point of view. Don't discourage them from offering ideas, but make sure they come from somewhere that has been thought through. With that done, every employee has the opportunity to bring their greatest value to the enterprise.

As trite as it may sound, the most valuable resource that any enterprise has are its ideas. Trained and highly educated employees are an asset. The structure of the building, the equipment, and the fixtures carry a paper value. The products and their features are very important. Goodwill, image, market position, history and culture all contribute to the measure of an entity to its consumers. Yet, all of this eventually goes away when ideas that move the company to a safer place in the long-term are not cultivated. It takes sharp minds to be competitive and relevant to the market.

Sound marketing is always based on having useful information that leads to good decision making while one is planning a course of action for a stronger business. Information is dynamic. Even with all the facts lined in a row, people make the wrong decisions. That could be because good strategic marketing is not the product of the kind of "if a equals b, and b equals c, then a must also equal c" linear thinking. People, the kind whose needs and wants vary so much that at times they may seem fickle and unpredictable, complicate the process. The problem is this: What is true to me, regardless of the facts that support the truth, may not be true to you.

We all recognize that "a fact" will support an argument or theory that can lead to sound conclusions. When we have enough facts we can set a course, plan a plan, and move toward a goal. Depending upon one's perspective, verifiable facts can be interpreted differently. What would be a solid reality in one perspective may not stand too much scrutiny in another. Some stuff that we know with certainty today, will one day be proven to have been wrong. Some truths have an expiration date. Chris Columbus didn't sail off the earth's edge and into a lair of dragons, nor is the earth the center of the universe. The transportation, communication, information management, and shipping models of a decade ago are not valid today. There's no promise that what you know today will mean anything tomorrow. That's why every company needs a real plan for the future. These plans should be born through the thoughtful cultivation of ideas from every level of the enterprise.

KNOW THYSELF

Perhaps the most extraordinary strategic success in the last quarter-century is the repositioning of IBM. It would have been impossible twenty-years ago to imagine them as the company they are in the 2000's. Up until the middle of the 1980's, IBM was the leading brand providing information technology through mainframe computer hardware, a pioneer in the emerging personal computing segment, and the supplier of office typewriters to the largest segment of the world's businesses. Its "Big Blue" image and IBM logo had value that placed their machines in almost every office of the global corporate community. With almost 70% of the market, they had no significant competitors. For the business customer seeking solutions, IBM became the symbol of stability and consistency, whose people came in button-down white shirts and blue pen-striped suits. They were a giant in their markets, and a giant among all other businesses in the world.

Twenty-years later, a large part of the hardware markets IBM once owned now belong to companies that compete head-to-head in a rapidly shifting paradigm of price erosion and consumer expectations for product performance. Removed from the desktops of offices around the world, they are replaced by machines branded by Dell, Sony, and HP that in the early 1980's were just emerging in the information management arena. These consumer-oriented products are promoted through the weekly sales flyers of the national electronics retailing and office product chains, discount internet sites, and many manufacturers' direct-to-consumer programs. A special offer promoted by a company one week, is trumped by their competitor the next week with more features, lower prices, and special value-added incentives. It's a head-spinning theater of market cannibalization that leaves every brand vulnerable to the lowest price of the day. Such an arena would make IBM's brand promise impossible to preserve. Selling cheap computers is not their business. Offering businesses the best value in information management is.

While IBM's outward appearance is so different today that even their starched white shirts have been retired, at the heart of the company's positioning, IBM was and still is a business-serving company. While the brands in the personal computing market continue to hammer features and value-added offers into the best consumer-value possible, IBM instead evolved with the business markets that meant the most to them. To focus where they were strongest, IBM stepped away from the price-driven PC market, systematically shed its poor-performing businesses, and shifted its identity from a hardware-centered company to a software solutions company that also sells hardware.

If IBM followed the practices of too many businesses, they would most likely be out of business today. When things are going well for an enterprise, it's easy for the time, energy and financial resources of the business to be inwardly focused on its day-to-day operations. If the bottom line is swelling, everyone lives better, capital improvements are made, operations are expanded, and people are hired. When times are tough, the entire enterprise looks with a short-term focus to turn things around. It's predictable for companies to lay-off employees, freeze hiring, cut promotional expenses, sharpen pricing, and myopically defend their bottom line. Regardless of whether business is good or bad, most enterprises lack the long-term goals of a strategic plan that all decisions could be filtered through. With a strategic plan, short-term decisions can be tested for long-term viability. Against the long-term goals of the company and the thorough understanding of its brand's value, abandoning enterprises that make no sense is easy.

During the 1990's, with its positioning and power, IBM did misstep. They were bloated with too many employees in a marketplace that was becoming less relevant to their processes every day. They were floundering in the personal computing game. Banking on their strength, size, and image, they eventually came to market with the PC Jr. Their push came with a fanfare of mass advertising on all the major media, and premium consumer product placements in almost every upscale department store. It was impossible to turn on a television and not see a Charlie Chaplin-modeled character pushing a baby carriage and miming his enthusiasm for IBM's new arrival. It was big, and public, and expensive. I had the occasion to ask a merchandising Vice President for Macy's in Atlanta how the IBM push was going and he told me, "We're selling a lot of baby carriages." People weren't buying the PC Jr.

For a brief period, the company struggled. Typewriters were being replaced by computers, so initially they fought to win that battle for desk space. Yet in the end, that was not their real battlefield. They were not a consumer product company and the personal computing business was evolving toward the mass marketing channels. As IBM re-stabilized, it came with six-digit manpower reductions and tons of negative headlines as job redundancies were addressed ten-thousand at a time in the newspapers. The changes came with a new CEO.

Louis V. Gerstner, Jr. took the helm of the company in 1993. He was an engineer with a degree from Dartmouth and his MBA came from Harvard. He had previously been the CEO at RJ Reynolds-Nabisco. It is difficult to imagine a better suited candidate for resetting the focus of IBM. The new CEO came from outside the organization equipped with the analytical mind of an engineer, a business education from a top university, and the experience of leading the strategic vision of a powerfully successful consumer goods company that, during his time there, had its own serious issues to overcome.

Under Gerstner, the IBM brand disappeared from most of the desks they once dominated. Yet, their position got stronger with many of the major businesses around the globe. Many companies in IBM's situation in 1993 could have been lured into believing that they sold hardware to businesses. They may have fought to their own proverbial death to keep their position on top of desks across the country. They could have been lured into the spiraling price war and its zero-sum position battle that would have consumed them.

Gerstner had a different perspective of the company's value to the customers it served. At no time in their 100 years was IBM purely a hardware company. They were always a business solutions provider. In the 1950's, those solutions came through hardware. Today they come from software. In 2004 (less than two years after Gerstner retired), the company enjoyed the most successful quarter in its 94-year history by booking $27.7 billion in worldwide revenues. The gross margin for IBM's software sales was 89%. How they meet the needs of their customer today is very different, yet the basic need they serve hasn't changed. In terms of their company's health, a market strategy that delivers nine-dollars of profit from every ten-dollars of revenue is far healthier than the low-margin, high-overhead hardware market they left to others. Every business manager needs to develop this type of understanding of the needs they address for their targeted customer. In a changing world, survival comes from anticipating how those needs will be addressed in the future.

IBM's actions were born from realizing strategically that the customer-base they served was not found in the Office Max aisles comparing laptop features. They realized their PC market position was not worth defending at the expense of the opportunities available by focusing on their core customer-profile. How would the image necessary for success in the company's multi-billion-dollar software-solution markets be supported by the price-slashing smiley-face at the local Wal-Mart?

IBM's agile adaptation to the dynamics of the market, the opportunities they discovered through its changes, and their understanding of the brand's value to the core customer in a new environment, is an important example for every business manager. Every business manager should understand clearly who they are and what they do for their customer that keeps their customer coming back.

Ask yourself, "What does my business do?" If the answer is "We sell internal combustion engines," your answer defines you in a way that could make you extinct someday. It fails to link you to a specific consumer need or want that you fulfill. When people no longer want internal combustion engines, you will be unimportant. If your company builds internal combustions engines for the racing industry, your answer might be that your company "helps to win championships" or "we sell speed." If you supply motors to the lawnmower industry, that's a better way to define yourself. What you do must be flexible enough to evolve with your customer. When you consider the identity of your own company, is it with the flexibility to still be viable to your current customers five years from now? Can you identify and cultivate the consumers that will be important to you in the next decade?

IBM practices a deep understanding of their customer by continuously meeting their needs and wants. The evolution from being a hardware-focused to a software-focused company may seem to be a re-invention of their purpose, practices, and identity. Yet, the company's core purpose since its inception early in the 20th century was to provide technology solutions for business. IBM knows who they are and what they want to be. They understand the changes within their evolving market and the conditions for success. They are disciplined in setting strategies that move the company toward their goals without significant distractions.

IBM reveals a long-term and short-term planning process that promotes innovation and risk measurement. The company even includes a strategic approach to personnel management and development that is centered on a dual-focused compensation plan for managers. They reward successful risk without penalizing short-term failure. Annually a manager is congratulated financially for their results, while promotions and position in the company are determined by their longer three-year production. Managers who fail are not fired, they are reassigned – the lessons of failure are too valuable to dismiss. Being a technology company, they understand that failure contributes to their corporate strength. In laboratory work, failures reveal information that before wasn't known. A manager that fails won't repeat the mistake and brings the value of lessons learned as an asset to the company.

The fact is most business managers fail eventually. Private entrepreneurs and large corporations can both follow a good idea into ruin. It's not always the ideas that are at fault. It's not always that there weren't enough customers for the product. It's not always because someone else built a better product or offered a more competitive price. Knowing the market, understanding the consumer, looking for a strategy within the shifting paradigm of purchasing habits and consumer opportunities is how survivors prepare and plan. The business enjoyed by the strongest and most enduring companies is not something that happens accidentally. It comes from thoughtful strategies and specific tactics that work to move toward the ultimate goals of the enterprise.

There are times when a business failure is due to external and uncontrollable influences. A hurricane, a factory closing, a closed highway exit, or a key supplier problem can be insurmountable for a business. Sometimes businesses fail simply because there just isn't enough time or money. You can have the best service and products, yet if the marketing ramp-up does not produce ample results to satisfy your cash-flow needs, the dream will be short-lived. Some businesses fall behind on the rudimentary management duties that could indicate trouble. Running a business takes time. There's always something to do that isn't being done. The easiest thing to put off is an honest and thoughtful look at the current state of the business and its markets.

Businesses are a lot like managing one's personal health. Just because your blood pressure and pulse are in check today, doesn't mean you can live a lifestyle that chain-smokes through the day and binge drinks through the night. Having the same strength and stamina in your middle-ages that you had during high school doesn't mean your body can process three-meals-a-day of pure drive-thru window dining. Good health must be maintained. Feeling well lures many to think there's no need to see a doctor. Of course, this is the surest way to miss a hidden medical condition before it becomes inevitably fatal.

The same is true for a business. When managers fail to manage the multiple tasks of running a business, including the tracking of results and regular evaluations of market conditions, they risk driving their companies to an unceremonious demise. A strategic plan maps a company's future. Without a detailed plan, the company has no defined route to identify threats and navigate through obstacles.

IBM demonstrates that companies proven to be successful over time in a specific market segment are not ensured a future in that market. Success, regardless of how substantial, does not make one immune to failure. Unfortunately, established entities are often tempted to get comfortable with their success and do not see a need to compete for, or defend their market. Internally and historically focused, their confidence can be largely the result of hubris, internal politics, or simply the lack of systems necessary to understand their customers well enough to anticipate their preferences and needs. By the time the managers of these entities realize the market is changing, they are too late to respond.

A company's resistance to change seems absurd when the surest truth in business is that markets are dynamic. Everything in a market is subject to change; the demographics, the cultural influences, the economic structure, the technologies. Every change brings a threat and an opportunity. Business is never blissful, regardless of one's position in the market. If you currently have a market position, someone will be trying to take it from you. If you fail to compete you will lose. If the field of competition changes and you haven't adapted, you won't succeed. How much should a company be prepared to adapt? Only the consumers for your products or services can tell you that.

When setting the direction of a company, the strategy for prolonged success is rarely found in defending a static market position one has earned with the consumer. Loyalty of consumers extends until the last time you meet their evolving expectations. As the culture and demographics change over time, so do the consumer's needs and wants. The consumer decides what and how they will buy. The key for protecting success, and perpetuating a company for decades, is to understand your consumers and to continuously anticipate and address their needs.

No company can depend on business growth. They can only plan for it with eyes wide open. Security and stability is not something you have, it is something you protect. Survival beyond the first good idea is dependent upon more good ideas. Companies compete to advance. To advance, they plan. To plan they must know their markets. Most importantly, they must know themselves – honestly.

The strategic planning process of many enduring brands helps them monitor competitive activity, cultural considerations, economic realities, and demographic trends. It is how they succeed in meeting consumer needs. They apply the right kind of thinking to ensure the questions they answer are the ones that need to be answered. They don't get mired in preserving who they are. They aggressively seek to be different, if different preserves their viability as the source their customers turn to for addressing well-defined needs or wants.

The biggest change in IBM in the 1990's, came when change was needed. Gerstner arrived with experience in the consumer goods industry. He was a "new hire." He took the post previously held by a homegrown CEO, John F. Akers, who led the company from 1985 until 1993 after being an employee since 1960. He brought a fresh perspective of what the company could become, and little of the emotional attachment that is inevitable in being a seasoned veteran of anything. He took the reigns and introduced the industry-neutral principles of consumer marketing that are the basis for survival in the packaged goods markets where brands are solidly positioned in the minds of consumers.

The formal strategic planning process introduced by Gunji at Brother is fundamentally the same as the one introduced by Gerstner at IBM. It is similar to the practices Gerstner brought from RJ Reynolds-Nabisco, and like those used by every brand you see in the grocery store that has owned the same shelf space for the last fifty years. It doesn't make you invulnerable. Most importantly, the formal strategic planning process accepts that you are always at risk of something and guides you to decisions that protect your company.

When We Get In Our Own Way

A few years ago I was flipping through the channels of my television set when I found myself watching the broadcast of a board meeting of an under-performing school district in South Carolina. A school board meeting isn't normally what one would expect to produce riveting entertainment, yet I could not change the channel.

What I found myself watching was the four kinds of thinking – intuitive, linear, mechanical, and strategic – all at work. I saw the kind of behavior that emerges when "knowledge" and "experience" give one the confidence to dismiss their weaknesses. The meeting presented a near perfect example of how refusing to recognize your vulnerabilities prevents improvement.

I had just flipped to the channel in time to hear a school board member ask the District Superintendent about the shortage of books he learned of from a constituent's call to his office. The Superintendent immediately explained that the actual problem was more related to "philosophical issues" than a real shortage. She asked the board member to describe the "magnitude of the problem" as it was relayed to him - it would be necessary to know how big the issue was before she was willing to commit resources to solve it. She assured the board member that the problems that they get in their offices are usually not accurately presented. The reply was impressive in its ability to talk around, but not to the question asked. She told him that if he wanted to know more, "You can direct your questions to the Cluster Superintendent" who oversees a smaller group of the district's schools. The Superintendent smiled as if the board member's constituent problem was solved.

"I'm directing my question to the Superintendent," the board member said firmly. He wasn't satisfied. He explained that he has gotten the same calls at the beginning of the school year, each of the three years he sat on the board. The Superintendent seemed surprised that the board member, after this explanation, still didn't understand how things were done. It was time to call the cavalry.

The Superintendent was joined at the dais by the "Centralization Coordinator," responsible for getting books in kid's hands. The board was assured that there was no problem. The Centralization Coordinator explained that each school had a "Text Book Coordinator" who reported to the school's Principal. The Principal was the primary point of control in the process. It was the Text Book Coordinator, working through the Principal, who is responsible for making sure that the books a school needed were purchased. She continued to speak of all the reasons why the board member should have confidence that nothing was wrong.   She spoke of the problem being caused by the combination of factors. Books are allocated based on the enrollments in the spring.   The district was experiencing expediential growth. There is a "replenishing cycle for the books."

She spoke for a very uncomfortable length of time, taking a very different approach than her boss, yet still saying virtually nothing that answered the question.   The board member was now a bit impatient. The students of his constituents didn't have books. The people charged with running the schools were satisfied that the system works. "Didn't you know the enrollment before school started?"

Through this exchange, the Superintendent and the assistant dug in, defended their processes, and asserted to the board that the situation has always been under control.   They were confident that the delay in getting books was not significant.   Their self-satisfaction was very hard to watch.

The human factors exposed in this exchange help to describe why this particular school system was not the shining beacon of progress in a state that ranked 49th in the country in educating their children. It also describes the kinds of discussions between salespeople and sales managers, sales managers and marketing execs, and marketing execs and CEO's in companies that are not progressing.

In this school board exchange with the administrators, the intuitive thinker was sure that the magnitude of the problem was overstated. "Usually the problems when researched aren't accurate as reported." It's a broad brush statement made without really knowing any specifics of the problem or why it came up. She had been in similar situations before and because it sounded familiar, she knew it was likely to not be a significant problem. Intuition doesn't require knowledge in order to make a person confident in their position. Their experience can lead them to the conclusions that make them comfortable.

Then the mechanical thinker explained, "We have a system. Don't worry." She answered without considering that the pieces weren't working together. Instead of an answer that focused on a solution, she described why no solution was necessary.

The educators in this scenario failed to realize that the board member, asking questions that a strategic thinker would ask, wasn't concerned specifically about getting the books to the kids. He was concerned that the kids didn't have books on the first day when there was so much information and time to ensure that they could. His question wasn't "How do we get books to kids that don't have them?" The question he asked was more strategic. As a member of the board of education in a poorly performing district in a substandard state, he wanted to know if this was why kids weren't learning. The answer to his question stood right before his eyes. Weeks later, the Superintendent was replaced.

Think of your own educational experience. Like many, you were taught plenty. But were you taught the skill of contemplation? Did you learn to question the logical conclusion? Did you develop the skills necessary for thinking progressively? Much of successful marketing is solidifying a sound plan in the "gray areas" where no one has gone before. Teaching children in school is basically a rote "one-plus-one-equals-two" process. To get an "A" you just need to have the right answers. Intuitive and mechanical thinkers can always find the right answer. The shortcoming in their kind of thinking is that it doesn't always address the right problems.

The manner in which we process information – how we think – is always going to determine the steps to resolve any issue. When creative solutions are needed, the capacity to organize the problems relates directly to how the problems are approached. Linear thinkers, intuitive thinkers, mechanical thinkers, and strategic thinkers are always in a position to influence outcomes. The strategic thinkers can be depended upon to reduce all the elements of a problem or opportunity to their individual parts and then reposition them to produce an advantage.

The District Superintendent in this example was unfit to lead because of an inability to think strategically – and as such she did not fit a key success factor for any sustaining enterprise. It struck me as a powerful example of how people with critical influence can derail any possibility of answering the right questions. The school board member said, "We have a problem." The Superintendent responded, "No we don't." Her subordinate employee stood at her side and confirmed there was no problem. What I wondered as I listened to the subordinate speak was, how would the conversation have turned if she told the board member, "Yes, we know the system isn't working." Quite likely, she would have been fired.

This scenario has value in the context of understanding how difficult it is to have a culture that allows things to change in order to improve. People resist the uncomfortable feeling that what they do is obsolete as the world changes without them. This District Superintendent and the CEO of General Motors share this trait. What they know gets in their way.

The change in leadership at IBM brought with it an individual who was not uncomfortable making changes in the company's identity, probably because he was not cultivated through it.   He knew that IBM addresses specific needs of a defined type of business client – and today it's why they are bigger and more successful than any time in history.   He came to the actions that repositioned the company by taking a strategic approach. The educators of the underperforming South Carolina school district gripped systems that didn't work and that served no one successfully, and as such, they contributed to why only two states in the US perform more poorly.   The educators had advanced degrees, experience, intuition, and lots of systems to confirm that all was going to be fine.   The great disparity between these two entities is how they think.

THINK STRATEGY

What was your company's last great idea? Where did it come from and how much did it make? How did it change the market? More importantly, what was its benefit to your company's long-term goals?

Something is always a threat. How we respond determines our fate. The tobacco industry reacted to early reports that their product could be harmful by executing public relations, legal, and laboratory-based denials. They employed lobbyists and advertising agencies. They used the opportunity for brand extensions like "light" cigarettes, with low tar, that were positioned to be "healthier" for you. They created their own studies to refute the damning facts printed in the medical journals. Yet, looking deeper into the activities behind the threatened brands, the companies also reinvented themselves.

When every product you sell has a message from the government that tells the consumer they're not very smart for buying it, you're going to have to be thinking of other things to do to make money. In elementary school in 1965, I made ashtrays for my parents when we threw clay into the kiln in art class. When I was in high school in the 1970's, we had a smoking lounge for students. In the 80's, attractive women would stand outside of the office building where I worked in Atlanta passing out free cigarettes to the passers-by. Today, if you're under 40-years-old, the clerk at the store may ask you for identification proving your age before taking your cash for the alleged killer.

The company that had once simply been called RJ Reynolds sells tobacco, for sure. But they sure aren't a tobacco company anymore. They executed tactics to defend their market position against a barrage of threats. They also realized that the power of societal pressures, largely created through unlimited public service announcements and legislation, required a more clinical approach. To survive, they needed to reinvent themselves. Before Gerstner moved on to IBM, he sold cigarettes. But as the CEO of RJ Reynolds-Nabisco, he also managed a bakery.

Strategic thinking is a very specific process that ensures the highest level of success with the information available. The right mindset of a strategic business manager is to think like a doctor. Think of your business as a life that depends upon your decisions. Think of it as a life that depends upon regular activities and check-ups to maintain and monitor its well-being. Few business managers adopt such a clinical approach to the planning and running of their companies. The health of many businesses is looked after in the manner much like the traditional image of a mother and her child.

When the health of a child is threatened, the mother might begin a course of treatment that was passed down from her mother. It's intuitive. The primary ingredient is hopefulness. She'll put her lips to the child's forehead to test for a fever. She'll ask the child how he or she feels.

Some company presidents choose to conduct business the same way. They'll see a dip in revenue and call the sales manager to ask, "What happened?" Like the child who has grown weary of the thermometer and would rather be playing hopscotch, the sales manager has to give an answer that defuses any suspicion that something could be seriously wrong. "I have a couple deals that will fall any day. We'll be back on track next week," might be the standard answer. He might even have a few details to give you proof that he knows what he's doing. Or, he might talk about how things are slow all over and that it'll all bounce back soon. Some of what he says might even be true.

The difference between the mother and her care for a sick child, and this example of a president of a company with an ailing revenue problem, is that the mother eventually takes the child to a professional if the things she does show no improvement. The president, on the other hand, is likely to start taking rash and reactive actions. He'll cut back what can be cut back and hold on until things get better. He'll put pressure on the salespeople to generate sales. He might lower prices to help. When that doesn't work, he'll start eliminating payroll. It's all a matter of time. The salespeople insist things will get better. Because they're in the field, they think they know. The folks in the Ivory Tower might recognize the revenue shortfalls as some historically predictable, market correcting "cycle," and take comfort that they know things will ultimately be okay. Unfortunately, this "half-full" glass of optimism is often just enough to drown a company.

When a doctor enters a hospital room, he or she will first pull the patient's chart from the end of the bed for an understanding of the real situation. After putting the chart back at the foot of the bed, the doctor might begin a series of questions and tests suggested by what the chart said. The reason the chart is at the foot of the bed is to keep the patient from reading it. It's to ensure integrity in the patient's answers.

No patient would allow a surgeon to start cutting without a thorough examination of the condition, an evaluation of possible treatments, and a chartable prognosis for success. Surgery only follows a rigorous effort to know everything possible about how the patient will respond. A doctor knows that sometimes a sore throat means the patient's tonsils need removing. The doctor also knows that every sore throat doesn't require such surgery. A smart doctor listens to what his patient says, but also runs an array of tests to confirm the information and to discover what the patient isn't saying. So should a business manager.

The president of a company should never ask his executives questions that allow them to invent an answer. Their answers should be filtered by the "charts," which should be based on the company's plans. If the sales reports show several clients with descending revenue trends, the president should expect not just an answer why, but the course of action to be taken to ensure the customer will be retained. A strategically managed company will have specific tactics employed at all times with measuring tools to evaluate the results of every progressive action. This should be the point of all discussions.

When there's an expectation not being met, the sales executive cannot have the privilege of reciting the daily news regarding economic trends. Hearing a sales executive talk about unemployment, social changes, the Dow, or some natural disaster is unacceptable. The marketing arm of the company should have set strategies and tactics with realistic goals within those conditions that would produce results. A president shouldn't accept surrender from his sales organization when faced with bad news. Like the doctor filtering a patient's answers through the charts, the president should be listening to what his sales organization is saying through his marketing plan, with an eye for finding solutions. If there are legitimate reasons for losing customers, they need to be re-projected in the plan, addressed in the budget, and tactics must be executed to minimize the loss.

Planning for known and expected revenue losses in specific terms gives the motivation to develop creative replacement strategies. Using the tobacco example, a sales executive setting his annual budget might typically pick a topside revenue goal that would show some acceptable growth that justifies his job. But that wouldn't be prudent. The percentage of smokers in the US is 2% less than it was a decade ago and just over half of what it was in 1941. The smokers also smoke less. The marketing-driven company would plan for the loss of customers that their market data predicted would be claimed by the Surgeon General. With this approach, the company will realize that depending on tobacco revenue will be detrimental to the company's health.

Nothing should be done to sell a product or a brand that isn't good for the long-term health of a company. This seems obvious, but businesses of all sizes frequently make rash short-term decisions before considering the impact on the company's bigger ambitions. Consider a few problems that managers have as they run their businesses from day-to-day. Suppose there's a target customer who needs your service but continues to do business with your competitor whose product doesn't do as good a job fitting their needs. Suppose your warehouse is filled with a pink version of your most popular model, but nobody wants to buy pink. Suppose a long-term customer decides to give some orders to your competitor, eroding the revenue you depended upon. Suppose you've had three months of sales that didn't meet projections. What will you do?

Think like a doctor. If you've never seen the problem before, what would you do? If you have seen the same symptoms before, does it always mean you are dealing with the same malady? If the malady is the same, is the cure going to be the same as you might have chosen for a different patient of a different age or general health condition. Everyone who has been in business has been in the situation where the top decision maker has deemed that the best way to create results is to cut something – price, payroll, products or services, or promotional campaigns. Such actions may eradicate an immediate symptom, but they don't always cure the problem. Like a surgeon, businesses that operate from a formal strategic plan, have the basis for diagnosis that guides you to cut only when cutting is sure to be the cure.

The answer for many of the problems in a business is to do what you planned. Good planning should anticipate most possible problems. If a problem comes up and a contingency wasn't planned, the answer to the next step in moving the company forward must be based on new information regarding why the problem needs to be dealt with in the first place. What don't you know? Why does the ideal customer not buy what you are selling? How can you lure him away from your competitor if what you offer is better to address their wants and needs? How can the stagnant non-selling pink goods be liquidated without disturbing the credibility of the remaining colors? What is your loyal customer telling you by testing the waters with a competitor?

The right answers to these questions are not going to come by asking the sales guys or kicking ideas around in the conference room. The solutions won't necessarily come by slashing prices, firing the salesman, or firing up a new promotional campaign. All of these might be the right answer. But before acting, you must first identify the problem with verifiable facts. When an employee suggests a solution to a problem without a thorough examination of the situation, that employee should be removed from the solution-creation process. If the employee suggests actions based on little more than hunches, experiences, or personal ambition, the best solution for the company's health is to render them harmless.

In marketing a business, those who are successful are informed and knowledgeable about the conditions of their marketplace. They understand what it will take to stay successful, and are willing to adapt and change to their evolving business environment. The opportunities uncovered through the strategic planning process, the confirmation of dynamics that dictate tomorrow's growth directions, and the actions that can change one's position within the order of an industry, emerge from the restless will to discover.

Like a doctor and his patient, a marketing professional's job is to maintain the health of a company and ensure its growth. The strategic planning process is akin to a proactive well-care program that monitors vital signs and stays alert to threats. It is the effective method that discovers potential problems so that they can be addressed in their early, non-fatal stages. Like the medical scenario, the doctor is always being updated with new techniques, medications, breakthroughs, and treatments to improve their results and reduce their risks. Could you trust a doctor that hasn't changed his methods of treatment since 1920? In the same way, it's silly to think you can protect the health of a company without updated and current knowledge.

A formal strategic plan keeps a company looking ahead of the status quo, anticipates technologies and cultural shifts, and keeps a finger on the economic pulse of a market. Consumer-focused, market-pertinent strategic planning ensures a company is prepared for change with thoughtful actions. Being prepared for changes in the market can eliminate hesitance to move in unpaved, yet potentially important, directions. A strategic plan removes recklessness from courage and allows a business to find prosperity by confidently charting a direction. Written strategies and tactics, with finite goals, will give clarity to the entire company. Every fundamental policy decision will have an outcome, and that outcome should be projected in specific language. The decision to move ahead should include some manner of reporting the results objectively. This assures that the facts about the market, consumers, competitors, and the company itself continue to be better understood from the results achieved.

If you have the capacity to think, if your brain hasn't been atrophied by rewards systems that discourage risk, you can be taught to successfully market goods and services to customers with needs. Marketing is a very specific process. It doesn't depend upon intuition, imagination, creativity, or guile. Marketing is as much a science as it is an art.

Just When Things Were Starting to Look Up

There's a plateau that every business reaches that too few young businesses have considered. It is as predictable as the morning sunrise, yet few new businesses find themselves prepared to address this eventuality.

Most businesses don't last two years. If they get past the early tests, they act as if they are "home free." Yet, every business, as it endures, needs to be aware of a specific customer type that has been called "early adopters." This consumer profile becomes the customers of new companies simply because it is their nature to always be looking for something new. There can be enough of these customers to churn through a business, to promote growth, and potentially mask a client retention problem. It could take as long as ten years before this customer profile is exhausted.

A new business marketing plan needs to have a specific strategy for the early adopter. We'll call them, "The low hanging fruit." Yet, there needs to be a justifiable investment of energy and dollars to get the ladder to pick some of the sweetest fruit from the top of the tree. Staying with the analogy, the future needs to be secured by planting a few seeds. During the first decade of a business, one can fool themselves into believing that what they are doing will work forever. It won't. Every young business plan must include an understanding of early adopters, a customer retention strategy, and strategies to cultivate all other customer segments that could benefit from your products or services.

You can't afford to get comfortable when all is going well. It's good to enjoy it, but time's test usually deflates the joy. Compare today's Yellow Pages in your town with the book of thirty years ago. Flip through the advertisements in *Time* from the 1950's and make a note of the brands and businesses that still dominate their markets today. Looking backwards, it isn't hard to see concretely how volatile every business is that isn't looking for the threats to its existence. We all drive automobiles, yet the place where we purchase gasoline is no longer the place where we turn for our car's service. Instead, it's the place where we buy milk, morning coffee, and lottery tickets. Electronic ignitions and fuel injection eliminated the old-fashioned tune-up and eroded the critical consumer mass big enough to sustain a service station on every corner. Tire centers and oil change specialty shops supplanted the old paradigm for attending to the most needed automobile services.

If you stand in the cereal or toothpaste aisle of the local supermarket it's easy to see whose practices are worth imitating. The packaging may be different and the product lines may have added additional line-extensions to defend shelf space, yet the brands that led twenty years ago still lead today. Colgate-Palmolive, General Mills, and many other companies keenly follow demographic changes, cultural shifts, technological advances, distribution and retailing evolutions, health concerns, legal issues and any other factor within their field of competition that will influence their ability to succeed. They keep a close eye on their competitor and have anticipated challenges to their footing with planned tactical responses.

If the manufacturer of your favorite breakfast cereal failed to earn your loyalty by anticipating what it is you are going to want when you walk down the cereal aisle, then you could become anybody's customer. It's their understood vulnerability that drives packaged consumer goods companies to do very sophisticated market studies to know how much of their cereal you'll consume, to keep them keenly aware of the competitive tactics employed to steer you away, and that ensures that they will have planned preemptive tactics to preserve your brand preference. They'll have a product plan, a packaging plan, a retail merchandizing plan, a pricing plan, and a promotional plan that are all balanced to tip your choice in their favor. Smart marketing is systematic. It isn't based upon habits that make a person comfortable, it isn't based upon experience, and it isn't born from past successes.

CHAMPIONSHIP MARKETING

It may seem obvious that a business manager that forgets to compete puts his company at risk. Yet, as you look at your own business, have you set aside a specific time for evaluating market conditions, reviewing your competitive position, monitoring your customers preferences, looking for your vulnerabilities and planning strategies and tactics to prevent them from being fatal? If you do set aside the time for strategic planning each year, how is the information you gather tested? How objective can you be about your company?

Those that manage businesses should borrow the habits of competitive coaches. If a coach managed by looking inward at his talent without considering competitive match ups during the season, he'd fail. If he were to try to keep a team successful by making all of his strategic decisions during the game, he would fail. If he allowed the players or fans to call all of his plays he'd fail. Regardless of whether you are the general manager of a professional basketball team, the coach of a high school football team, the CEO of a major corporation, or an entrepreneur selling knishes on the curbs of New York, the level of success and security of your endeavor is directly related to your preparation.

Vince Lombardi, the legendary coach of the Green Bay Packers (and for a brief spell, the Washington Redskins) started every season the same way. At his first practice he'd assemble the veteran players, coaches, and hopeful prospects together, hold the inflated pigskin in his hand and say, "This is a football." To players who excelled in the game his action might evoke a laugh or puzzled look. Yet this ritual was his way of preparing the team for a work-style to which they may have not been previously exposed. Lombardi made the point of identifying and presenting each element of the game in its most basic form. His methods ensured no player could be confused about what was expected of them, or their role in securing the team's goals. As the person responsible for building the success of the team, he wouldn't assume anything was properly taught to the players he acquired, or remembered by the players he coached the season before. "This is a football." This is the way to run. This is how to block. This is tackling. He started with the most basic elements, moved players past their personal experiences and press clippings, and created the environment for engaging them in his evolving vision for the game. Nothing was taken for granted. He defined the team's objectives clearly to everyone that could influence the outcome. He didn't buy into the axiom that "practice makes perfect." The coach said, "Perfect practice makes perfect."

John Wooden was the same. As the legendary coach of UCLA's basketball team, he started each season by teaching his team how to put on their shoes. It is something most players in college have done for themselves since their fifth birthday. But it also was an important part of his game instruction, and a reminder to veteran players that their feet are the foundation of success. No detail of their game was overlooked. He set strict standards for the team to eliminate distractions. Sure, Bill Walton could keep his hair long, but if he did, he wasn't going to dress for games. It was a basic process that understood every game created an opportunity to fail, and that is was his responsibility to position them to produce the highest degree of consistent success.

In general, coaches of professional sports teams devote most of their time to being prepared for success. They scout the other team's tendencies and plan to make the most of their talent against them. Sports competition is a very visible environment affected by dynamic changes that can influence where the team must focus to succeed. As seasons go on, the coach will fine tune the game plans and devise game preparation tactics. If a player gets injured, the coach devises the best contingency for success. Field conditions, weather, competitive strengths and weaknesses, game tendencies all go into a comprehensive plan to win. The competitor's methods, habits, and preferences are known as well as possible. Coach Lombardi never assumed anything as he prepared his teams to be successful. You shouldn't either.

Without making a purposeful effort to know everything possible to generate success, you are at a disadvantage that makes you incalculably vulnerable. To engage in competitive commerce without understanding the conditions of the contest, would be like Vince Lombardi going an entire season without considering there might be a threatening response to his plans to win.

The extent of planning in too many sales-driven companies is to add up last year's business and factor that total with a fuzzy plan to do more. Yet, it is faulty thinking to assume the customer-base you serve has loyalty beyond their last order. There's always something your loyal customer needs or wants that they are not getting from you. Don't assume that good service and low prices are enough to keep your customers coming back. It's important to know why people do business with you, but more importantly, it is critical to understand what other needs they hope you will be able to address. It is more than wise to be paying attention to the competing companies and how they are gearing up to steal your customers – regardless of how big you are and how strong your presence is in the market.

When you go to your office and turn on the lights, how can you be sure that the lights will continue to go on? Every business manager should realize that when the lamp glows across their desk it represents a simple victory over rivals who want to take their business and dim their lights forever. How can you keep them on? What is the strategic direction? What are the tactics? How will you continue to successfully compete? Is there a game plan in your top drawer?

As the world changes, the strategic planning process is how new possibilities and threats are revealed. It ensures companies notice the changes where they do business and ask, "What can my company realistically become in this environment?" followed by "What do I need to be doing in order to be prepared for long-term success?" In a bottom-up business culture, the directors become vigilant to outside threats that emerge and are prepared to preempt them with relevant and meaningful tactics. The line-level managers never take current success for granted and constantly seek information that gives a clearer view of the course. Business managers doggedly test the assumptions upon which their business decisions are made. Their goal is to work from information that is current and proven.

It's generally safe to say that the brands in *Time* ads today, which were also found in the magazine pages during the 1950's, have survived because of the formal planning processes that set their long-term strategies. These processes can be adopted by any business in any market. The general process for formal strategic business planning is the same whether you are selling artichoke hearts or artificial hearts. Formal strategic planning provides the structure for accountability, disciplines for uncovering changes, and the framework for thinking. It doesn't present answers, but it does provide a way of finding them. More importantly, it helps to ensure you are asking the right questions.

Strategic planning does not provide absolute crystal ball solutions for profiting from the dynamics of a market, nor does it guarantee that you will be successful. It's a discipline. To be useful, it requires an honest approach that looks urgently outward for new and relevant opportunity, and not inward to rest on past successes and experience. Inward vision must be diagnostic. What's wrong? What can be better? Smart planning is systematic and patient.

Identifying the opportunities, threats, and obstacles within a market is critical to understanding how to guide an entity into the future. Being too close to a situation, being steeped in experience, or depending on established habits and traditions may obscure the collective vision of a company's managers. It may prevent an enterprise from seeing the obvious. Factor in human qualities such as personal ambition, politics, job security, and fear of failure, and it can be completely blinded. The formal strategic planning process can provide the tools that force decision-makers to step away from their daily tasks, and realign what they believe they know with the verifiable facts they must know.

To develop a successful strategic plan, a company must be willing to discover things about itself it may not like. Strategic planning puts a company in the right frame of mind for questioning its decisions and revealing what is necessary to perpetuate growth. To be as inwardly objective as the process demands requires courage. It requires an emotional disconnection that many business environments find challenging. Think of it as being similar to a doctor that has to make a troubling diagnosis on his own child (which is why doctors don't usually treat their own families).

Intellectually, every business manager understands that technologies evolve, cultures shift, consumers change, competitors sharpen, distribution shuffles, and successful companies adapt. Emotionally, too few are willing to see the warts and vulnerabilities that their competitors will ultimately exploit. It doesn't matter if it's a pizza shop, a muffler shop, or The Home Shopping Network, if you expect your business to weather the years and grow continuously, there are things you will need to do someday that you aren't doing today. It takes an honest evaluation of current conditions to make this happen.

Strategic planning can frequently reveal knowledge that disturbs conventional thought within a company. That's why companies should always be prepared with tested documentation to verify all information upon which their conclusions were drawn. With verified facts and tested information, the debate regarding any decisions or actions can't be personal or personally threatening.

Where it is practiced effectively, "marketing" serves a company the same way the Intelligence Department at the Pentagon serves national security. Marketing is about evaluating threats and allocating resources based upon probable outcomes. Marketing is to research, test, and know the current conditions of the market in order to discover opportunities and claim a stronger strategic position. Of course, marketing professionals are also responsible for propaganda, but only as a component of marketing's broader definition.

At leading branded goods companies, ideas are hatched through research. They could come from a hunch, but that hunch is substantiated with a verifiable and defendable analysis of current conditions. No product sees the light of day at leading consumer companies unless they address specific consumer needs and wants, provide measurable product advantages against the competitor, and fill a defined gap in the market. The product itself is rarely enough to lead to success. It must be able to be produced, promoted, and delivered to the customer at a price and frequency that is profitable. It must be able to sustain itself under competitive pressure.

Experience has a value, but in almost every environment it is advisable to not depend upon it. Pick just about any product and consider the changes in its distribution over the last three decades. What are the experiences that would have made an IBM retailer successful in 1975 that have relevance today? How have consumer habits changed for automobile manufacturers during this period? Marketing is about surviving and requires that no one be allowed to say, "This is the way we do it." The marketing process helps identify the changes a company needs to make in order to defend or gain leadership.

PLANNING TO PLAN

Among the biggest challenges in setting a formal written strategy for a company is making the time to do it. Every company has non-believers at every level that would rather be using the time "more productively" than plotting a course that they already are sure they are on. The facts, however, can emphasize that the best use of their time is to use it to plan. Statistics state that when people in a business merely say they will do something, they achieve it only 5% of the time. The probability that goals will be accomplished increases as they are written down, shared, and tied to specific measurements. When put into a formal written structure with a deep understanding of the marketplace's dynamics, specific actions, projected results, and regular reporting, the probability of success exceeds 80%.

In order to ensure the planning process is productive, it must include specific elements. The parts of a complete plan are: Goals, Current Conditions, Key Success Factors, Strategies and Tactics, Financial Projections and Plans, and Critical Assumptions.

All elements of the strategic plan should address the components of the marketing mix: the place, product, price, and promotion of the brand, products, and services. All information against which decisions are made should be footnoted with the source and date. No part can be built on experience and guesses. When "Place" is considered, it should understand and take into account the human factors of the people in the marketplace, the people throughout the distribution channel, and the people within your organization who may influence the outcome of the company's efforts.

To set the strategic planning process in motion, it's often a good idea to block off time and select a place away from the distractions of the regular functions of the business to get started.   Include anyone that has value to add.   The ideas in this planning process should be recorded in a way that nothing is lost.   The first question to answer should be, "What do you want the company to be in five years?"

It's impossible for a strategic plan to have value if every element is not well defined.   The goals, the key factors for success, and the strategies and tactics should be quantified.   The acronym SMART has been used by marketing experts to remind them that everything in the plan should be: Specific, Measurable, Attainable, Realistic, and Trackable.

Defined in specific, measurable and realistic terms, a strategic plan must begin with the ultimate objective or objectives of the company. A goal must be stated in very definable and measurable terms.   For example, if a professional minor league ice hockey team sets attracting more families as a goal, it needs to be stated in language that specifies the number of families set as the target, and it must include verifiable measurements to monitor progress.   When Hiromi Gunji said Brother International would grow to generate a billion dollars in annual revenue in the United States within ten years, it became a measurable ambition for the company by specifying how much and when.   When John Kennedy promised a moon walk before the end of the 1960's, there was no question of what would happen and when it would take place.

Goals must be realistic and fit the conditions in which the business operates.   The minor league hockey team couldn't realistically set a $1 billion revenue goal and Gunji couldn't expect to put a Brother employee on the moon.   Looking at Brother International's market position and size in 1984, one might have thought that the ten-year, billion-dollar target of a company with $200 million in revenue was outlandish.   Perhaps in the context of the company's history, it was. Yet, against the evolving market conditions and the company's capabilities of the day, it wasn't.

When goals are specific, they focus the tasks of the company on the achievement of very specific results. Goals can be determined by need. In the case of Brother Fax machines, goals were based on the minimum marketshare necessary for the company to stay in the fax machine business. A minor league hockey team may set its goals based on the financial realities of staying afloat. Ideally, goals should be tied to opportunity. We can go to the moon, so we should. We could be a billion-dollar company so we will.

Brother provides a very good example that separates the value of market-driven and sales-driven business planning. Brother's key competitor (who at the time was the market leading brand) responded to the state of the 1980's typewriter market by moving its production out of the US in order to reduce production costs. They were fighting for a share of a shrinking industry, which was in effect, investing good money for a shrinking opportunity. Brother saw the projected opportunities in the future of the market, and realized that survival meant the company needed to be redefined. Ironically, today they also hold the remaining typewriter spot in most consumer retail channels.

Current Conditions

Current conditions can change rapidly. A stable environment, regardless of how long it has seemed unchanged, can swiftly be altered, leaving the unprepared in ruin. Understanding current condition is to look inward *and* outward. It is to identify a company's strengths, weaknesses, opportunities, and threats (the SWOT analysis) with an honest and verifiable assessment of the situation. It is to understand the competitors, consumer trends, financial realities, and internal needs of the company. It evaluates staffing and payroll, taxes and legal issues. It digs past the obvious and sets the stage for the remarkable.

Running a business is never blissful. Someone or something is always plotting to take your marketshare. Threats must always be addressed in the plan. Too often, businesses of all kinds operate without knowing the various conditions that can influence their success.

Failure can come from many directions and long-term, sustainable success rarely comes from a "good hunch."

Identifying the opportunities of a business through the strategic planning process clarifies the mission. Thinking militarily, a detailed strategic plan will help to focus efforts at the points where the battles won will alter the balance of the larger war. Like the General committing lives to gain advantages in war, before pressing on toward its goals, a company must have an honest evaluation of its own strengths and weaknesses.

How are you currently performing? Describe your customer-base and why they are your customers. What potential do you have for growth? Which products are most successful? Why are they selling? Do you have products that under-perform and why? Is there adequate and affordable manpower with the skills to do the necessary work and provide a consistent standard of performance? Does the company comply with local laws and federal regulations? A business must be sure there are ample sources of revenue available and that cultivating them can be done profitably and within the budget.

The decision-makers who guide a business must correctly identify the size of the total market and the companies that are engaged in it. What benefits are consumers seeking that you can address? What are the distribution channels that you will use to reach the consumers of your goods and/or service? You need to know as much as possible about the business model of each of your distribution channels. You must identify the competitive pressures you will have to address to be successful. Can you identify your competitor's strengths and weaknesses, and describe their areas of vulnerability? Everything you believe must be verified and proven.

Before committing to a strategy, it is important to know how to position your products and/or services against the competitors. Organize the information by price category, list all valid features and specifications, and describe their benefits and unique value-propositions.   Model-by-model, segment-by-segment, know who has the strongest products regardless of their market position.   Identify who the leaders are, and track those who may be growing threats. What is the current financial position of your company against the competitors? What are the competitors' strengths and weaknesses? Is there the capital necessary to endure difficult times, and are financial resources available to support growth? With the correct knowledge, your successes in achieving stated goals are best assured, regardless of your size or the competitive order within your marketplace.   Think strategically and act systematically. David would never challenge Goliath to a Wrestlemania Cage Match.   He'd strike strategically, with actions that bring the odds of winning in his favor.

The story of David and Goliath is retold through the systematic, focused, and patient targeting of the US market by the Japanese auto producers.   Never imagining their vulnerabilities, the US automakers lumbered along with confidence and certainty through the 1960's. Yet, armed with an understanding of the field of competition, the smaller competitors slung one rock at a time.   First they stunned, and then they crippled the giants.   Eventually the monuments of American power were left to die.   With artificial life support they continue for now.   Yet, even with breath, there hasn't been much evidence of unique and innovative positioning to prove that they aren't brain dead.

From Japan, we were able to see the kind of systematic and thoughtful long-term approach that can work for almost any business and any industry. In the 1970's, Japan attacked the Detroit machine where they failed to understand the consumer's wants.   Initially the Japanese manufacturers introduced subcompacts to fill a product gap in the market.   Then they brought values head-to-head against the core automobile profile.   After gaining a position in the mass-market segment, they introduced luxury lines and prestige brands.   Looking forward, the threats continue to rise in an attack on the Big Three's final stronghold.

The US producers, led by Ford, have had an historic grip on the truck market.   They should, after all.   Trucks are the ultimate symbol of American ruggedness.   I recently sat at a stop light next to a "Ram Tough" Dodge with an imposing footprint, a snorting "Hemi" engine, and a window sticker that boasted, "My Lug Nuts Take More Torque than Your Foreign Truck Makes." Yet, anyone paying attention knows that the icon for the rugged individualism of the American male psyche was taken to task in the most public arena possible.   In the premiere All-American motor sport, NASCAR's Craftsman Truck Series, the winner drives American-made Toyota trucks.

As systematically as the Toyota exploited the US manufacturer's vulnerabilities in the retail showroom, they are now widening their presence in NASCAR.   The Toyota brand has been attracting championship teams and drivers (like Joe Gibbs racing) to their campaign in NASCAR's premiere car racing series.   If the old, "win on Sunday, sell on Monday" charm of NASCAR holds any validity today, the future could make every Monday a bleak one for the truck and car retailers of the US brands.

By carefully attracting one new customer segment at a time, the foreign manufacturers have steadily eroded Detroit's grip on the American consumer, invaded areas where Detroit had been strongest, and revealed the Big Three's leaders as out-of-touch and myopic.   The labor unions exposed their employees to a job competition that includes a more appropriately compensated workforce building cars with foreign nameplates right here in the United States.   The foreign competitors came here to beat the American automobile producers in a systematic, thoughtful, and calculated showdown that was based on learning how to position their strengths against the competitor's weaknesses. With a "slingshot" approach they got their start by serving the niches that Detroit ignored.   Success in these niches parlayed into a threat that the US producers didn't imagine possible.   It opened the position in the consumer's mind that also allowed them to accept products from Germany, Korea, and Sweden.   American's now prefer the cars that these foreign invaders build.

Paying attention to the kinds of cars that occupy the roads from their homes to their offices should be ample research for the Big Three auto producers to realize they are not doing something right. Unfortunately, one of the hardest challenges in setting a bottom-up, market-dictated strategic plan is to separate one's self from the traditions and pride found within the walls of a company. A company's financial position, its manpower and resources, its growth trend, its retention of customers and sponsors are all to be defined objectively in the analysis of the current conditions in the formal strategic plan. Current conditions should present an outline of the agreements and relationships with suppliers, the local business community, and media with a measurement of their value. It needs to know why people have done business with you and why they may or may not come back in the future. It should accept that your competitors do threaten you and will take your customers. Yet, few have the courage to look so objectively at themselves.

I once worked in a company where formal strategic planning was briefly attempted. As the information was collected to present a crystallized picture of the current conditions, I discovered that the database of the company's customer information was inconsistent and incomplete. That led me to realize that there was a rift between the outside sale organization and inside sales support personnel – each refusing to enter data because it was the other's job to do it. I also uncovered that the company had surprisingly few active customers, and very few repeat customers. Commissions were being paid to sales-people for business they cultivated through subcontracted vendors who were also being paid commissions. I discovered several more grave self-caused vulnerabilities the deeper I dug.

The executives, and most of the company's employees, functioned with confidence knowing their industry posted a trend of 20% to 25% in growth for a decade or more. Yet, in the specific segment of the industry on which this company focused and identified itself, the growth trended at just over 1% each year throughout the previous twenty years. Their confidence was based on a myth. In fact, their share of this growth was at risk because the product they offered was out-of-step with the accepted standards established by the market leaders in the segment. However, there was a silver lining to this depressingly dark cloud.

In the initial stages of the planning process, I found over a dozen advantages that the company had in a segment of the business that they didn't focus on. Without any change, other than a repositioning of their product story, they had advantages that would set them far above the industry standards. When combined, these strengths created an undeniable value-proposition that could reposition the company for greatness. The unique position the company could claim prompted strategies and action plans that were realistically capable of generating new revenue, expanding the customer base, and elevating the image of the enterprise.

This was all very interesting to the company's President, but it was new territory for him. The first step he took was to stop any further work on the strategic plan. He thought it was interesting stuff, but he explained that the employees didn't want to change. The second step he took was eighteen months later when he laid-off employees because the company wasn't producing self-sustaining revenue.

To everyone in the company (except the CFO) this planning process was a waste of time. Actually, most of the supervisors and staff members that were included initially, worked the initial stages of the planning process beautifully . . . up to the point that they had to commit and be accountable to specific action plans. This scenario was not unique to this company.

I have seen it plenty of times. The resistance to having a formal plan is that people sometimes must change what they do, how they see their company, and they must accept a level of accountability that makes them uncomfortable. However, the strategic planning process should actually give employees greater comfort because it produces nothing vague. It reveals, identifies, and clarifies what is happening, what will happen, what can happen, and what must happen to keep them from being a victim in the battles for commercial viability.

For a company to head in the right direction, it is not enough to understand the markets currently served and the segments being missed. To talk about attendance of a hockey game, for example, it is important to understand how many tickets are being bought the day of the game, the week before, and how many seats are filled by season ticket customers. It has value to know the key identifying characteristics of each segment. That will give you a basis for modifying internal behavior, and will bring added focus toward better service to the customer's needs and wants. Knowing age, sex, marital status, and ethnicity will reveal successes, failures, and opportunities. This can be invaluable in honing your marketing and improving your results with the various consumer profiles in your market.

It can be fatal for a business manager to make decisions based on faulty or obsolete information. A sales manager for a distribution company once stated that people did business with his company because of their "low-pressure" sales approach and "high-level of customer service." It is what he wanted to believe in spite of the statistic that over 30% of his customer base fell off their books each year. Instead of recognizing that the pragmatic reason most customers did business with his company had more to do with the COD payment terms, same-day shipping, and their "no minimum order" policy, he clung to something un-measurable in terms of strategic goals. It was a self-satisfying and fuzzy illusion around which he could wrap himself. He ignored the reality that, once credit worthy, these customers moved on to competitors that offered them payment terms regardless of the warmth and pleasant experiences they got from his staff.

The reason a significant segment of his customers engaged in commerce with him had little to do with service, and everything to do with the fact that few other companies would honor their orders. This was not a bad basis upon which the business was built. But to think it was built on something else could be dangerous. It prevented him from focusing on the reasons he had customers in the first place, and inhibited the ability to improve where the company's values were strongest. Clinging to his favorite myth, he fundamentally impeded finding strategies to increase customer retention. With the wrong understanding of who the customer was, his company eventually was led to its demise by initiating competition in segments where it had little standing and few competitive advantages.

Doing current condition research with due diligence moves you past your educated guesses and faulty assumptions. When Brother took its facsimile strategy to market, they didn't invest in building a large consumer pull. There were no magnanimous expositions like the Macintosh Super Bowl ads of 1984 to shift their position from a fraction-of-a-percent of the market to its top position. They didn't court masses of consumers through the pages of the magazines on the newsstands. They focused on changes in the distribution channel and relied on selling just a handful of people: the buyers of the strongest retailers. Identifying the changes in the retail merchandising landscape, they saw where their opportunity would be found, and then focused on the factors that would make them successful.

Reviewing current conditions routinely as part of the planning process does not only keep you abreast of changes that you may have already observed. It establishes the vehicle for investigating their implications.

Key Factors of Success

Understanding the Key Factors for Success is a lot like planning a vacation. In order to enjoy yourself, and for the trip to be successful, what must be in the suitcase? How much money will you need? Is your passport current? Are there adequate opportunities for transportation that fit your budget? What kinds of things will ruin the experience if they are not available or managed? This analogy makes a significant point regarding the importance of planning strategically for business. Most people spend more time annually planning their vacation than their business. They know there are risks that could ruin a holiday if the itinerary is not thoughtful.

Without defining the tangible, specific, and measurable elements that must be in place for a successful franchise, a company cannot be sure it understands the environment and may not be able to chart its success within it.   In professional ice hockey, a key factor for achieving bottom-line profit goals may be the kind of venue lease necessary to function profitably against the threshold of the ticket price and the number of tickets to be sold.   A key success factor would identify elements that must be in place to draw fans and to provide them a consistently positive game experience.   It would describe the factors required for successful promotion. It would detail transportation issues, concessions, and other elements that make the experience one that a consumer would want to repeat.   A key factor of success will quantify and confirm that there are enough commercial sponsorships and advertisers to be realistically gained for the team to succeed.   It will quantify and ensure that the season tickets that must be sold and retained are possible.   Key factors determine the difference between success and failure.

Strategies and Tactics

The next two components of a strategic plan work hand-in-hand.   In order to reach the goals of the plan, it takes a strategy.   Strategies are executed through a series of tactics (also called "action plans") that when combined, achieve the goals of the company.   Strategies are generally drawn from the current conditions of the market.   A tactic is the specific action taken that is drawn from the strengths of the enterprise and focused to ensure the highest probability of success. Studebaker in 1959 saw a product gap in the market and developed a car to fill it.   The strategy to develop a car to meet an untapped market was sound.   In retrospect, the tactic to use the retailers of the Big-Three manufacturers to reach the consumer was not the best long-term action plan.   It was not drawn from the company's strength in the marketplace.

A football coach may study his opponent and discover a tendency or weakness, which if taken advantage of, could turn the game in his favor. Maybe he sees a rookie cornerback standing in for an injured all-star. His scouting and films will confirm the cornerback is slow but has an exceptionally high vertical jump. The current condition suggests directing plays in the slower, inexperienced player's zone. That decision would be a strategy. The action plan would be the specific plays that isolate the weakness to produce positive gains for the team. Strategies and tactics do not always reflect what a coach *wants* to do. They are the courses and actions a coach *must* take to improve his results. The coach must only respond to opportunities and conditions, and do so with the best actions to meet the goals of the team. The same is true for a company. To engage in a price-war with Wal-Mart is foolhardy. To recognize your strengths against their vulnerabilities (and they have many), and to focus on the markets that will enjoy a personal benefit from your value-proposition, is prudent.

Good strategies are meaningless if the tactics are not effective. At Studebaker in 1959, the strategy was to reach the emerging two-car family with a dependable, economical, and affordable compact vehicle. This was a solid product strategy that delivered immediate results. Yet, they discovered that there is more to marketing than having a good product. The tactic that they executed was flawed. Bundled with the other miscalculations they made since the start of the 1950's, they were well on the way to their demise.

By acquiescing to union demands, which created payroll and pension obligations for the company that could not endure through increased competitive pressure, Studebaker's management started a series of financial problems. Bolting Packard body parts on Studebaker frames didn't serve anyone's needs or wants and created significant customer retention problems. Putting the innovative compact cars on the lots of the Big Three retailers begged for a swift and aggressive response by the brands that established the traffic to those dealers. In the isolation of the moment, these were all good ideas. Yet, any action of an enterprise that is not focused on the ultimate long-range goals of the company, and mindful of the potential vulnerabilities they might bring, is a waste of resources, a misdirection of energy, and often the beginning of the end.

Forecasts and Management Tools

A formal strategic plan is not complete unless it contains the financial plan of the company. If you're planning successfully, you will be able to quantify your efforts through anticipated results. You may have objectives that are defined by the sales of specific units, marketshare growth, or increased transactions. You may plan for a growth curve that will come from tactics that increase revenue from the current prospect base. You may draft strategies and tactics to be successful in specific un-served gaps in the market. You might see specific revenue to be gained from key customer targets. With the plans set, you should be able to translate the results into product sales, inventory needs and time constraints. Once top-side revenue is projected, the expenses to support the success should be detailed. The facilities, utilities, manpower, freight, postage, insurances, promotion budgets, professional fees, and anything else essential to growing the topside revenue should be included.

Putting the strategies and tactics into financial projections reveals the revenue necessary to record a profit and the cash necessary to serve the demand. It may identify the need for new strategies and tactics to reduce expenses, generate faster cash flow, or inject new money into the company. If your strategic plan identifies revenue opportunities and those revenue opportunities are based on the sale of inventory, you would be wise to plan your inventory needs to ensure the cash is available to serve the demand.

This is where the rubber hits the road. You can only achieve revenue from what you can deliver. If yours is a service business, the skilled manpower available that can provide your service limits your top-side revenue opportunity. If it's a product you must inventory, your facilities, cash flow plan, and credit line may present a growth limitation.

The financial elements of the strategic plan must be complete. The ability to meet critical financial demands will make or break your company – income, gross profit, expense control, available credit, and cash flow. Every strategic plan needs to be tied to these financial elements to ensure that success is realistic.

Critical Assumptions

Things like top side sales, cash flow plans, inventory turn over, and gross margin projections will be based on certain assumptions regarding the available market, the ability to borrow, the products, and the competition. Increases in interest rates, labor strikes, legal or cultural changes, will alter results. A strategic plan should list anything assumed, which if changed, that could alter your results.

Planning is Crucial

The benefits of having a written plan (and the risks for not having one) emphasize why having a formal strategy for every enterprise is crucial. Finding the time to plan, and to do the work necessary to ensure it is comprehensive, can be the biggest challenge for any company. But it's worth it. Why? Because when you commit your objectives to a plan, do the work necessary to ensure they are realistic, and establish regular reporting points to track your results, you can increase your chances for success by 1600%. If you just say you'll do something, it will happen 5% of the time. It's worth repeating - when an objective is committed to a plan with a formal structure, it happens over 80% of the time.

WHEN THE STARS ARE ALIGNED

I once happened to pass a small church on a back road in South Carolina that had a slogan on their placard that said, "If you have done everything else possible, prayer will work." I actually turned my car around so I could be sure I read it correctly.

As wise as this message was about prayer, it was equally profound as a statement for marketing. When so few businesses succeed and so many products fail, when economic changes influence our ability to compete, and when we are challenged everyday by forces that want to dim our lights forever, we need to be thoughtfully prepared in order to survive. In the profession of marketing there are occasions when all of the elements of the mix fall together so perfectly that it almost seems like luck. But luck is the by-product of a thoughtful observation of the real conditions in the market and sound planning to address its opportunities. Without proper planning, a business doesn't have a prayer.

Among the category leading products that I have launched, one was catapulted to its leadership position by a solid market penetration strategy - and a chance conversation regarding the condition of the market with someone able to help pull it the rest of the way. We'll call the conversation a prayer answered.

When Groove Juice (the leading product that drummers now use to clean their cymbals) was first introduced, there was a significant challenge in every level of the marketing mix that needed addressing. The product itself was far and away a better performer than anything else the industry offered. Yet, the established process for cymbal cleaning was too much work for it to have become a necessity for the typical drummer. Tarnish and the other elements that accumulated in the grooves did not dull the sound enough to invest a whole day of elbow grease and mess that was inherent in cleaning them. As a result, carrying cymbal cleaning products was not a priority for retailers. Customers didn't ask retailers for this kind of product. Enter Groove Juice.

Groove Juice was a technological breakthrough. Rub it on, rinse it off, and cymbals looked new. It was easy to use and produced a result that would appeal to any cymbal owner. Drummers would certainly buy this product if they knew how well it worked. The challenge was finding a way to credibly get that message across to the market.

An ad promising that "this is the easiest product ever to use" would be met with cynicism. Actually, even if it were three times as easy to use as the leading product of the day, it wouldn't have much appeal. Most drummers didn't clean their cymbals because they understood that the work to do it was difficult and the return wasn't worth the effort. As such, drummers were conditioned to believe they didn't need this kind of product. They also were not gullible enough to believe everything they read in a magazine advertisement. Other factors presented challenges, too.

Getting dealers to stock the product would be an uphill battle. For the few drummers that did care about the appearance and performance of their cymbals, the market already had an established leader. There was no need for the retailers to disturb that position for an unproven upstart. "What do I need this for? Nobody is asking for it," they would say. The current top-selling product cost a lot more money. Why would they take a small niche product and simply trade the dollars downward? It's an understandable attitude that the wise retailer adopts to protect their cash flow. The retailer is not responsible for building the brand. They are simply the conduit to the consumer. Bring them the customers and they will fill the need.

Unfortunately, even making the retailer aware of this exceptional product was problematic. With the exception of a handful of retail chains and high volume stores capable of buying in case lots, the majority of music stores are of the "mom and pop" variety that buy their accessory items through regional and national accessory wholesalers. Some of these wholesalers serve the retail market with field sales personnel, and others use a bank of phones to make outbound calls by the hundreds. It is a business of replenishing the thousands of established consumable small goods. Some wholesalers stock over 10,000 items from guitar amplifier tubes to xylophone mallets. With a deep inventory of goods, the salespeople of the wholesale companies that keep retailers in-stock with their key accessory items would not be inclined to devote any energy to sell an $8 bottle of cymbal cleaner. The time taken to "pitch" this magic fluid might only earn them just a few nickels for the effort. There was no justification that could make selling it worth while.

The reality of the situation was that even if the retailers did buy the product, it would likely die there. Music product consumers have specific brand preferences. They arrive at the retail store with brand names on their lips, be it Dean Markley Strings, Dunlop Picks, Vic Firth Drum Sticks, or Horton Valve Oils. The size of most accessory items tempts shoplifting. The shopkeeper typically keeps these items merchandised under a display counter or set on a back shelf behind the cash register. To discourage pilfering, only a few items ever make it to the counter tops where they can be accessible to the casual shopper. If the stores stocked Groove Juice, it would be stuffed behind the counter until a customer asked for it.

However, in the instance that a shopkeeper had the goods in-stock and gave the item merchandising attention, success could be virtually guaranteed. A retail salesperson in the music products business can serve the factory in telling a product story better than any other advertising or promotion medium. They have the influence to spread the good word on a product at the point-of-sale while the consumer is in a very agreeable buying mood. If they like what you make, they'll sell it.   They also have the strength and power to kill any poor performing product.   They have no reluctance to pass along a negative experience – whether they actually had it themselves or not.   The good news was that Groove Juice worked as well as its promise.   If Groove Juice were to get the endorsement of the salespeople on the retail floor, they would quickly add the product to the list of add-on accessory sales to any qualified customers with whom they made contact.   "Here are your Pro Mark drumsticks.   Have you heard about Groove Juice?"

In short, there was a lot to deal with that got in the way of the new cymbal cleaner's potential success.   Groove Juice was a product that the consumer was inclined to believe they didn't need.   The retailer would be interested, but the consumer needed to be asking for it before they would tie up any cash for the product.   Unless the dealers are buying, the wholesale salespeople aren't interested.   You could spend thousands for a campaign that would reach an end-user who was already too jaded by the over-promising of the typical advertising message that he wouldn't even notice it.   Even if you got them to the store, the advertising would be wasted because the dealer wouldn't have the product in-stock.

Yet, with Groove Juice, we had seen that when a drummer tried it, they bought it instantly.   They recommended it to other drummer friends. It took one demonstration of the product to win over prospective customers.   Like the door-to-door Electrolux salesman or the cookware demonstration in the mall, seeing the product work would make sales. The product was irresistible.   It would sell in great quantities if there was a practical means of getting it in the hands of the user.

To be successful, Groove Juice needed to create a consumer buying habit from a latent consumer need.   The consumer's negative predisposition regarding "cymbal cleaning" needed to be erased and replaced with a more welcoming view of "cymbal maintenance."   The trick was to find a way to get the consumer to try the product.   The challenge in pulling all the pieces together for a launch plan that addressed all of these conditions was daunting.

To get things rolling, the company invested in a budget to send two-thousand, two-ounce bottles of the magic solvent to drummers that subscribed to *Modern Drummer*. The most read publication in the category, *Modern Drummer*, features profiles of significant artists, player techniques, equipment maintenance articles, and product reviews. The magazine shares the life experiences of artists who their readers emulate. It improves the reader's playing skill with meaningful lessons and performance tips. It tells their readers about the products available to help their performance lives.

We sent these active *Modern Drummer* subscribers a small parcel that included enough Groove Juice to clean one cymbal and a promotional piece that described the range of consumer benefits. "We knew you wouldn't believe how well Groove Juice worked unless you could see for yourself." An advertisement appeared in the magazine, hitting the newsstands at the same time the bottles were received in the prospective consumer's mail.

The leading consumer brands have used this kind of strategy to sell laundry detergent and shampoo for years. The tactic was perfect for the product the same way getting you to try the "new and improved" laundry soap might change a buying habit. With a couple thousand consumers exposed to the product, they started going to retail stores for more. The results were immediate. Foot traffic brought retailer support. Retailer support brought showroom salespeople telling the Groove Juice story. Business ramped up swiftly. It was satisfying, but that was just the beginning.

At the same time the mailing campaign was launched, a quantity of the cleaning solvent was sent to *Modern Drummer* for a product review. After testing the product, the editorial department of the magazine contacted me as part of the routine fact checking process. The reviewer was completely impressed. He said something to the effect that "It works just like you said it would. Everyone here is crazy about the stuff."

I shrugged, "And that's the problem we have." I confided to the editor that sales could be stronger if only there was a way to get more retailers to stock and sell the goods. I explained the dilemma that dealers won't stock accessory items that consumers aren't asking for. Ads claiming "greater, better, easier" have been used to sell everything for so long that the consumer is jaded and skeptical. No matter what the company said in the ads, it wasn't going to generate consumer pull. The effect of a few thousand sample bottles of Groove Juice was strong, but not enough promotional dollars were available to push sales to their maximum potential.

The brief conversation with the editor was open and honest. It was mildly risky. Product reviews can be a dicey situation. They are subjective. They can be very "nit-picky" because the magazine's credibility hangs on each word. Unadulterated truth of a product reviewer is paramount in maintaining the magazine's loyal readership. As it turned out, this conversation became the difference between a fairly good business with a slow and steady growth curve, and the instant spike and sustained consumer acceptance that the brand now enjoys.

When the review of Groove Juice finally hit the pages of the magazine, it was a glowing testimony for the ease and effectiveness of the product. The solvent was objectively tested on several different brands of cymbals and varying degrees of tarnish. The results were very appealing. It was the kind of review you always hope for, but rarely get. Drummers would notice.

"This may be the best $7.95 you will ever spend," the article said. It told the readers that if their favorite retailer didn't carry the solvent, they should get the retailer to call the supplier. It listed contact information for the reader to take to his retailer. It was very direct, something like "If your retailer isn't carrying this product have them call. . ." It listed toll-free phone numbers and addresses. The results catapulted the cleaner to the top of the category by a large margin and led to its eventual acquisition by Pro Mark, a leading drumstick and accessory manufacturer.

This was marketing.   Step-by-step it addressed all the elements in a way that met the strategic goals for the brand.   It identified a range of current conditions and went directly to the root-challenge in stimulating sales.   It understood that the product was the best of its kind, but also recognized that such a fact alone would not make the product successful.   It asked the right questions.   It didn't attempt to solve problems it couldn't and as a result the campaign was remarkably efficient.   It wasn't at all about flooding the market with consumer advertising that skeptical prospective customers would ignore.   It wasn't about pushing goods through channels that don't respond to pushing.   It was a complete campaign that reached the segmented consumer target, influenced them through public relations, delivered the promise of the brand, and altered their buying habits.   It was effective because the product itself needed nothing more than to be used to be believed.

Most significantly, the planning process identified the greatest obstacles and invested adequately (but no more than necessary) to address them.   Every allocated dollar worked to achieve a specific goal.   The basis of every action was an honest assessment and correct knowledge of the current conditions.   Every tactic answered a key success factor revealed through an understanding of the key market conditions.   It was clean, controlled, and focused.   Every second invested in planning paid off.   Every dollar spent was justified.   The planning was strategic.

PEOPLE ARE DANGEROUS

I once was engaged in the kind of discussion with the account executive at an advertising agency that reminded me of the old adage, "you shouldn't argue with a fool, because people watching may be confused by who is who." At one point he tried to bolster his argument by stating that he had a "Masters Degree in Marketing" and "graduated with honors." I'm sure he did. Maybe he got it from a moderately good school. I'll bet that his term papers were all perfectly spelled.

Here's an appropriate analogy: Just because "Rudy" was on the football team at Notre Dame, it didn't mean he was qualified to play for the Green Bay Packers when he left school. In the same way, the individuals with the analytical skills that produce the best results in the strategic market planning process are not as common as the number of individuals that went to school to acquire those skills. We are *not* all created equal. Just as there are distinct types of thinking, there also are varying capacities for thinking within them. Some people are smarter than others. Some have the aptitude to resolve complex problems. Some can see information and understand what it means in ways that may not be obvious to others. Simply stated, folks who know what they are doing, prove themselves by doing.

In business, there is no validating argument for non-performance. This advertising agency's account executive was surprised that I wasn't impressed enough by his exceptional wall of degrees to keep him on a retainer. He was shocked that the awards and honors his firm earned through their clever advertising campaigns didn't move me. I could not continue retaining him because all of the expensive promotional investments that were supposed to deliver results arrived empty. To make fixes in the work the firm presented always involved protracted, and almost circular, conversations that ended up being recorded as billing hours for which I was invoiced. The more their work didn't meet our needs, the more it cost us. They could print their own money and not do as well.

By my gauge, there was only one measurement for this firm's value to my company. How did their work increase our revenue? How did spending for their cleverness at the rate of $175 per hour, plus the commissions tacked on to the actual cost of the media buys, pre-press, and printing they orchestrated, increase my business' strength? Which campaigns that earned awards and trophies actually made my company healthier and positioned it to be more competitive in the future?

Imagine going to a restaurant that served up a platter of mashed potatoes with a fly in the gravy. If the cook came to your table and told you about his culinary training in France, and the manager brought over a certificate with the health inspector's highest rating, would you pick around the fly and dive right into the mashed potatoes? No, you'd probably look at them and say, "Yes, but there's a fly in my gravy." Actually, you'd be smart just to leave.

Advertising agencies that do not produce measurable profits to your company haven't advertised anything useful to you. They are a drain on your budget, not an asset. Paying for their services should be considered in the same way that you pay your salespeople. If they produce, they have a value. If they don't, they need to be terminated.

Of course, there are also a lot of people with "Sales" written on their business cards that really don't fit the definition. Salespeople that do not produce sales are not really salespeople. They are a drain on your resources and a threat to the opportunities-at-hand. Their preparation, the things they say, and the presentation of your value-proposition, defines your company. The impression they make will linger with the prospects they fail to sell.

Every time a salesperson tells your product story to qualified prospects, and your products and services are more excellent than your competitor's, they should close the deal. If they have a reasonable opportunity to produce results and they don't, they are killing your company, damaging your image, and opening the door to a competitive threat. Selling is a science. It has steps and structure. When the process is followed with discipline, salespeople produce results. If your salespeople are not selling, they probably don't know how. Maybe they haven't been taught how. That doesn't mean they are bad people. It just means they are bad for your business.

The point is this. The best marketing plan is at the mercy of the quality of people serving it. Untrained and obtuse salespeople cannot compete against the trained and brilliant. Being smarter than the next guy can win some sales from the competitor, but it is not assured if the competitor is better trained and is working a plan. Salespeople in a strategic marketing environment should be carefully managed. Their primary function is to execute the marketing strategy. Letting the sales organization drive the direction of the company, as often happens, allows the "tail to wag the dog." They are "in the market," but their market knowledge is often false.

By their nature - and by the methods they are motivated, compensated, and monitored - the salespeople within most organizations cannot be objective about the strategic balance necessary within the marketing mix. You want them in the mindset that encourages them to perform. The marketing arm of the company should be in a position to create the environment for salespeople to succeed by understanding what the customer needs, knowing how what you offer fits in the competitive environment, and providing them the tools that make them successful.

By being "in the market" and compensated with rewards based on "what have you done for me lately," when the competitor drops his price, any salesman worth his salt wants to drop your price. The competitor launches an ad campaign. They want to spend more on advertising. It's a reactionary viewpoint that clouds the picture. They are people – and as such they can have biases, experiences, and firmly held beliefs that are slow to respond to market changes. The information they provide can have great value. But it only has value if tempered within the long-range mission of the enterprise, and it reflects the current dynamics of your world. The things they might want the company to do may have been designed in real time to increase revenue in the moment. Sometimes that is good. Sometimes, it might not be.

In many environments, the people creating programs for the sales organization have no idea what a salesperson's life is like. They forget that the people forging forward with the company's mission are humans that need to be supported and encouraged, a fact that truly underscores the main vulnerability of a marketing plan. The success and failure always comes down to "the people" that touch the plan and who the plan touches.

When the "Four P's" principle was first introduced to describe the marketing mix in the 1940's, many suggested there should be "Five P's." Some said, "Packaging" should join Product, Place, Price (Profit) and Promotion. Others suggested "People." I've thought for most of my practicing career as a marketer that the original four were adequate. Isn't packaging included under the umbrella of promotion? And people - aren't they part of "place?" Yet, I've adjusted my view. People are far too important to not earn their specific focus.

The people – the prospective customers and the people that influence the plans of your company - should be considered as a "P" as independently and as broadly as possible in the marketing mix The people within your organization and throughout the distribution chain should be understood. The people that surround you and your ambitions also need to be considered carefully. Attention should be paid to their motivations, and how they think, so that the plans the company puts into motion are compatible. Do you have the right people internally to meet your goals? Are they in the right positions?

In reviewing a company's strategic plan and its progress, it is critical to evaluate personnel. This needs to be based on specific objectives and with the flexibility to appreciate that when things don't go well, it may not be the person that has a flaw. There could be something mistaken in the plan's reasoning. But it must also be done with a keen awareness that some employees are not good for the company. Some are well-meaning, but they are still a dangerous drain on the health of the enterprise. Caution needs to be taken to be sure that no one with an influence on the plan becomes complacent – in good times or bad. Having specific and formal methods for sharing expectations with employees is necessary or you really have no right to expect anything. Weeding out those that do not bring a benefit is tough work. It is emotionally taxing. There are lots of lovable incompetents.

At the top of every company sits a person that may have no connection with the work being done to support his position. It is natural that their focus is on regular sales and financial reports that keep tabs on the company's vital signs. Yet, that creates a disconnection that should be corrected without the equally problematic alternative of micro-managing. A formal strategic plan that includes a management-by-objective review of personnel and their objectives is a start.

Personnel management and employee accountability needs to be strategically overseen with tactics to ensure productivity. Every hire has a job, every job has a structure, every structure is designed to meet an objective to ensure a value is gained and goals will be met. Without such definition, it is possible that employees can be mishandled, their importance under-valued, and their efforts can be overlooked. At times, it has been known that a company's chief (who is in his or her position because of big-picture vision and innovation) has pulled manpower from their more urgent duties to chase whimsical brilliance. Without having each employee, division, strategic business unit, or project team constructed around specific strategic directions, the active imaginations of the company's leaders will follow the advancement plan of an ameba.

Several years ago, when the phone company assigned a new Area Code to the town where I worked, the boss of the company decided that the new area code presented a hot opportunity for punching up revenue. We were a vertically self-sufficient wholesale distribution company with its own graphic arts department. The boss decided that all of the businesses in the area would need new letterhead with the current and correct information – "So let's go do that for them." He couldn't suppress his enthusiasm for the unlimited possibilities of generating this new revenue. He saw the opportunity to turn an expense line of his company into a profit center.

Meanwhile, his business was churning out $175,000 a day in wholesale accessory sales from over 9,000 items. As he put this idea in motion, a consideration of the workload the graphic arts department was bearing was not part of the process. The small staff of four produced over 2,000 pages of advertising production every year, took all of their own photography, and drafted every syllable of advertising copy. They willingly put in evening hours and weekends in order to meet the deadlines of their department. Additionally, during peak seasons they would be called from their duties and deadlines, set their skilled professional graphic arts training aside, and work in the warehouse a few hours a day to pack orders in the company's non-failing effort to keep their same-day shipping promise to its customers. The boss' new and exciting "revenue opportunity" merely created an emotionally deflating burden for the department. It confused them and made them wonder if there had been any consideration for their skills, talents, and education. They were behind schedule. They were already being pulled from their priorities and juggling home-life against the department's demanding deadlines.

This kind of management is endemic of a sales-driven business autocracy that does not have the machinery in place to sift good ideas from the bad. Wouldn't the energy be better focused on increasing revenue where the company was expert? Could the few hundred dollars of typesetting revenue make the company stronger in the long-term? Against the other demands of the graphic arts department to support the core business, wouldn't the effort to cultivate and serve this new business be disproportionate to the potential gains? A single page produced to support the company's market objectives reached thousands of customers with an engaging message that produced revenue. The same energy applied to fixing the stationary of the businesses in the community would take as much time, produce a few hundred dollars of revenue, and have zero impact on the company's mission. How did this revenue generating vision focus on the long-term needs of the company? Frankly, it didn't.

Focusing on the specific goals a company sets out to accomplish is paramount to being successful. The opportunities that pop up along the way must be weighed against the bigger objectives. Sure, if you can grab a few quick bucks and have the capacity to do so without diverting attention from something more urgent, you should. But usually, such distractions are insignificant against the test of the company's real mission.

In daily business management, distractions and short-sightedness are common. Why invest any resource – whether it is your cash, manpower, or goodwill - if it doesn't support your long-term and short-term plans? Why have energy pulled away from the key purpose of your mission if it does nothing to improve your position?

Without a formal strategic plan to channel the focus of all employees, (including, if not especially, the boss) there's always an opportunity for spontaneous inspiration and knee-jerk reactions to take place without a method for filtering their priority, weighing the value of their return, and understanding the long-term consequences. If the strategic plan of the company is thoughtful and complete, anything that detracts from it by pulling resources, shifting attention, or confusing the ultimate objective can be resisted. This is not to say that ideas shouldn't be encouraged. A strategic plan is not a manner of flying on auto-pilot. It is a formal document with specified goals, which if met, ensure the success of the company. The big picture aspect of the plan gives it priority over everything else, and makes it the basis for filtering that which is productive from that which is not.

The boss thought it was a good idea for his talented and experienced staff of graphic artists to be pulled from their more urgent demands. He was banking on an opportunity that came to his mind on the drive to the office that morning. The boss saw money to be made, thinking intuitively, and not filtering the idea through a strategic process that validates its value in helping the company achieve meaningful progress. It added stress to an already stressed group of skilled employees and presented no real way of improving the company's strength and stability.

Having a formal plan provides managers a valuable filter for their ideas. Ponder how often you hear people in a meeting open their mouths and say "I think" when there's rarely much actual thinking behind it. They mean to say, "I feel" which is an expression that has no value to marketing. Always challenge those who say "I think" by asking "Why did you say that?" To a strategic marketing specialist, the whimsy behind "I think" is a dangerous threat to a company. They're fighting words to any defender of the company's future. The gravity of every marketing decision must be understood before any steps are taken.

Of course, while the answers given to "why did you say that," occasionally expose fools, you must listen for brilliance. The regular challenge to discovering useful information is getting past your own obstructive assumptions, experience, knowledge, and commonly held beliefs, to discover what isn't known. Human nature and personal comfort can get in the way. These are internal dangers that can be found within a company's culture that need to be neutralized. The right strategies for long-term success can only be discovered if allowed by the company's culture. It's natural for education, experience, ego, politics and individual ambition to influence the development of a business' plan. Inexperience, impatience, and laziness can creep into the process, too. Arrogance and ignorance can be the root of bad marketing. These human factors can result in a disaster that costs people their jobs and upsets their lives.

The people that drive a business must be engaged and committed to its success. That could be the strongest argument for bottom-up management. There was a management quality about Hiromi Gunji at Brother that didn't make an impression on me until years after I left the company. I always knew how he wanted the plans to be structured, how he wanted presentations to be delivered, and the depth of detail he expected to support all positions. Yet, as I recall the times when I was putting together the formal plans for my area of responsibility, I remember that I never had any idea what he expected to see in terms of content. Unlike the guy I mentioned earlier who was justifying the location for his corporation's move, when I went into Gunji's office I didn't ever know figuratively "where he wanted to live." He expected to be presented a plan that made him confident in the operation of our division and the positioning of our products. He wanted to know how we were going to run our divisions and why we made the choices we did. He wanted to be sure we had the long-term focus that was in-step with his.

To act without a strategic long-term focus you may make fatal errors. Brainstorming to find swift solutions that are prompted by falling short of the goals on a "this-year versus last-year" sales report rarely address a core problem. Actions that are decided in these conditions rarely focus on the end game. These solutions can be generated in a vacuum of panic and often will have the power to compound the problem at a future date. The brainstorming question usually answered is "How can we hit this month's numbers?" The questions that should be answered are: Why is revenue down? In what way is our strategic marketing plan out-of-step with our goals? What don't we know?

Marketing guru, Peter Drucker, believed that when you have a good marketing plan, selling is superfluous. When the business you are doing is not meeting the expectations of your plan – when the battles for marketshare and other opportunities that you planned to gain are lost - you should be asking why selling isn't superfluous. What core issues did you miss? These questions often point to a "people problem."

The quality of any plan is irrelevant if not matched with capable, knowledgeable, educated, trained, and experienced people. But that alone is hardly enough. They also need to be smart enough to make sound evaluations of the information at hand. They need to be flexible enough to let go of obsolete beliefs. They need to be agile enough to adapt. Having the strong sense-of-self that removes ego from the business planning process is critical to productive results. Everyone that is involved in promoting the ideas that move the company forward should be restless competitors, with a clear understanding that they are absolutely vulnerable, and that every action has a consequence. They must recognize that regardless of the times and conditions of the market, someone is winning, and that those wins could be at their expense. Good planning with great execution ensures every opportunity is exhausted.

The legendary John McKay, the original coach of the expansion Tampa Bay Buccaneers was asked after a loss, "What do you think of your team's execution?" He replied, "I'm in favor of it." Championship marketing requires having the right people to realize the plans. If your ad agency isn't making you money, fire them. If your sales organization is not in-step with the results you need for survival, fire them. If the leaders lose focus and begin acting as if tomorrow is assured and there is no vulnerability that needs to be addressed immediately, fire them. A good plan is only as good as the organization's ability to see it through successfully.

WHERE WILL YOU WORK TOMORROW?

Let's discuss the core purpose for strategic marketing. Ask any schooled marketing graduate how the text book defines marketing and they'll regurgitate a well rehearsed reply. "Marketing is providing goods and services to the consumer systematically and at a profit." I've heard it said a few different ways, but always, marketing as it is defined is no more difficult than figuring out how to make money by selling people stuff they want. But, there is always a greater purpose. Marketing is also about sustaining a healthy enterprise so that the company will endure. At Southwest Airlines – a company that has bucked the struggling trend of its industry - the "cause" of the company is "to increase the collective prosperity of all of the employee family." As the company's written purpose, it shapes the decision making process. It gives a long-term test to assure all of the solutions to its problems (and all opportunities on which they focus), will bring an enduring benefit. It gets right to the heart of why we must succeed in our businesses.

The advantage of being a marketing-driven organization is that the structure consistently provides the framework for long-term strategic decisions. When there is no long-term view, the wrong questions are often answered. Having an answer to a problem, whether it is the right answer or not, can produce a sense of satisfaction that something is being done. Without a long-range vision, we can be happy with our answers even if the answer obscures the real question that should have been asked and prevents an opportunity to reveal the right solutions.

The CFO of your company may see a drop in revenue and ask, "What can we do to boost sales?" To make an immediate impact, perhaps the answer is to create extra incentives to focus salespeople, develop a volume purchase incentive for the retailer, deliver the goods with value added incentives, and to execute a three-pronged promotional campaign using print media, broadcast media, and an internet campaign to generate traffic. With all this activity augmented by strong point-of-sale merchandising support, you could possibly create a spike in top-side revenue numbers. Salespeople might load their customers up in goods. The masses will see the promotions that are intended to make them take an action, and they will head to the stores to make the purchases you need from them. Eureka! Sales are up, the CFO is happy, the plan showed genius.

Suppose two months later, the CFO is at your door again. Over his shoulder is the CEO. "What can you do to generate some revenue?" he asks. You know how easy it is, so you tell them not to worry and get their blessing to launch the same approach that you executed two months ago. They smile. They may even go to lunch together to enjoy the anticipated success. The plan to move goods and services would surely kick up the sales numbers.

Unfortunately, the initial reaction a couple months before was not based on a systematic marketing plan. So, this time your salespeople may return from customer meetings with their tails between their legs. The genius demonstrated two months before only answered the question that would produce a sales spike for the P&L report. It didn't answer the question that needed answering.

Maybe in his rounds, your competing salesperson noticed the growing inventories of your goods with his customers. He may have asked what was going on, and the smart merchant (working both sides of the street), filled him in on your campaign details. In reality, the campaign didn't really solve anything but a short-term sales problem for your company. That's a game two people can play. The merchant willingly shared the details of your program with your competitor, who then met every one of them with a better offer. When your multi-pronged media campaign moved consumers to go into the store to buy your product, they were diverted to the competitor. Equipped with the same plan two months later, your salespeople didn't make sales. They returned with retailer requests for product returns, mark-down dollars, or advertising funds to deal with their bulging stock problem. Because the company's marketing plan didn't ask the right question in the beginning, now you are in quicksand.

Every management professional should honestly and constantly question the thoughtfulness of their decisions. They should create the framework so they can be questioned by others. The key problem demonstrated over and over in management isn't that people don't know how-to-do, it is that the model for operating business doesn't demand that they think about the long-term consequences of what they do.

Growth in business is anything but comfortable. The expression, "growing pains" was born from this fact. Among the art hanging in Hiromi Gunji's office at Brother International was a framed ink drawing in Chinese calligraphy that defined the Ten Spartan Rules. Next to it was their English translation. I only recall Number 7 – "Never avoid conflict. From friction comes energy." The message is simple, when the markets are dynamic and every enterprise is absolutely vulnerable, what you have done before has no bearing on what needs to be done today. It is vital to have the energy that comes from change.

Change never comes without friction. Sometimes the friction is caused by the resistance-to-change by employees that are comfortable with their jobs, know and do them well, and just want to be left alone to collect their check until it's time to retire. Sometimes the resistance is prompted by a fear of the unknown, new levels of accountability, or a redefinition of the work that could shake an employee's confidence. The person closest to the tasks may resist because they have a different perspective. The friction they create is the kind that might add meaningful improvement. In any case, the clearest truth in business is that most fail. The world changes with every turn and the companies that survive are the ones willing to create the energy that is required to keep pace with it.

It's logical to expect a company to fail when the driving force behind the enterprise is the experience of its managers. Businesses may die in two years because of cash flow. They may die in ten years because they have churned through all of the early adopters and lacked a plan for cultivating more permanent customers. Those that die in twenty years may do so because they missed the nuances of a generational change, were turned obsolete by a technological advancement, or were lost in a cultural revolution. There is only one proven way to guide a company through all of these challenges. The president that avoids the strategic planning process has, in his actions, also abandoned the company's future. Smart company leaders know that change rarely comes without friction – and resistance to change helps make it more perfect.

There is a work style that keeping a company healthy requires. If every company operated as if they were absolutely vulnerable, there would be one question every employee with an influence in its course would ponder on their way to work. "What can I do today to ensure that my company will survive until tomorrow?" Without the advantage of a plan (one that is based on understanding the dynamics of your marketplace and how your strengths best address them for your growth), how sure can you be that the doors of the place that you depend upon for your income will be welcoming you inside when you arrive? How can you be sure they won't be barred with security officers there to turn you away?

To get back to the point, the definition of marketing is absolutely functional for those with some level of finesse. It's that key word "systematic" that tends to trip up those without the capacity for strategic thought. From time-to-time we should remind ourselves that marketing isn't about what you do today. It's about the planning of your business objectives in the framework that makes today possible and tomorrow probable. The financially-focused management group that came from the aircraft business to run Studebaker was focused strictly on quick returns and streamlining expenses while they battled to work their way out of receivership. They were good at both, practicing their expertise right to the company's end. Focused on short-term survival, and answering the day-to-day challenges with quick solutions, they operated with little vision for their future potential.

The obtuse, the lazy, and those who feel too comfortable, tend to discount the value of a systematic management of the complete marketing mix. There's a short-term, in-the-moment stupidity that shallow thinkers might glean from the text book definition of marketing. So let's toss out the definition so often misunderstood. Marketing is not about selling goods and services. It is a structured process and a fundamental necessity to ensure a company has a long-term future from selling goods and services that are thoughtfully positioned for their best possible success in the marketplace.

The real purpose for making sales is to ensure that the company survives. It's not gimmicks. It's not about shooting your wad at a problem that only comes up because you initially didn't rely on a thoughtful and information-based understanding of current conditions. The "fun and wacky" persona of Southwest Airlines is a distraction in a culture that is starkly serious about their responsibility to the lives and livelihoods, the families and communities, and the supporting companies that depend on the soundness of their planning and decision making. In contrast, if the typical line worker in the auto industry gave regular thought to the volatility of the company they depended upon, that they invested their future in, that held their pension, and that oversaw their health care program, they might never sleep comfortably again.

Imagine how it could be possible for the omnipotent post World War II American automobile industry to be caught so off guard by the Japanese manufacturers at the advent of the first gas crisis and the consumer's growing concern for the environment. The CEO at General Motors lived in the same changing world as the leader of Toyota. The research and development group at Ford was a lot closer to the emerging Baby Boom generation than the R&D group at Nissan. How could they allow their market to be penetrated so significantly?

Of course, an American with faith in our greatest business icons would assume after the Japanese's initial strike on the automobile industry in the 1960's and 70's, that it would be unimaginable for America to be beaten to the draw ever again. It would make sense that the lesson from this attack would be learned so well, that the Detroit powers would be ready for anything that ever arose in the future that would jeopardize their market share. Detroit would certainly respond with a bold and aggressive strategy to reestablish its leadership. The action plans would hit with power. The Americans would send the Japanese home wondering why they did anything so foolish as to take on America in America.

After the initial attack on the US market, it would be logical that Detroit would always be the first to deliver the kinds of products the market would be demanding. Hybrids and electric cars would stock the Big Threes' showrooms long before they appeared under a Toyota or Honda marquee. You would think any organization of quality – certainly organizations with the resources and vitality of GM, Ford, and Chrysler - would be addressing their problems with a long-range focus, minimizing any weaknesses, fortifying their strengths, and crushing the foreign invaders. Unfortunately, the key weakness that Japan took advantage of had nothing to do with the products produced by the Americans.

The Japanese positioned their ingenuity to strike American hubris squarely between the eyes. Even against eroding marketshare, the culture of the American automobile manufacturer has not accepted that there may be a better way to plan business. They still develop products in a vacuum that fall behind the pace of the imports. The Japanese and German auto manufacturers are way ahead in delivering to the genuine wishes of the consumers. Instead of investing in technology to address the real needs and wants of consumers, Detroit

175

compensates with zero-interest financing, "guaranteed gas prices for a year," rebates and other marketing gimmicks that the prudent find insulting. Instead of following the dictates of the consumer's expectations, they repeat their sins again and again. The Big Three sell cars. The foreign producers win their marketshare by filling the transportation needs and concerns of consumers. They approach the American consumer with solutions that have been divined from research that tells them who the Americans are and what they want an automobile company to give them.

While this is a book about marketing, I'll confess to having distain for the pop culture's expectation that reading books can open one's eyes to a reinvented self. Frankly, there are no instant solutions of a "one-minute" management style or a list of habits to ensure your success. You can follow all the personal lifestyle habits listed in the plethora of books that promise the secrets of success, and still fail. You could publish such a best-seller and follow your own advice into bankruptcy. "Chicken Soup" is good. But the soup of business is not made from chickens. Business is anything but canned. It's about dynamic knowledge. Success requires the willingness to change, not just once, but every time the market tells you to change.

People who will get the most from this book are the people that see business as something beautiful. The Japanese businesses that I worked with in the 1980's gave me an opportunity to see business practiced as if it were an art. They understood the marketplace as a canvas and created something meaningful on it with the tools they had. Success came from discipline and commitment. It was cultivated through knowledge, insight, training and vision. Success in business begins with an uncommon aptitude and an innate ability to process and interpret information. You must be smart to survive the game.

There are a lot of product and service ideas out there. The people who think them up naturally believe their ideas should make them rich. I promise you that the idea isn't quite enough. Clever isn't the fuel for a successful product, service, or business. Neither is hard work, timing, price, or a big advertising budget. There is no advice that can instantly teach someone how to be successful. Being taught through educational opportunities, the blessing of a gifted mentor, experience in the right environment, and by reading the right kind of books can be invaluable in helping prepare for success. But success is really only the by-product of actions substantiated in current knowledge which exploit opportunities in a changing world. It won't come from imitating, nor is it safely delivered through dependence on past experiences and historically accepted practices.

The basic tools of successful marketing are an adequate IQ and the personal fortitude to look objectively – without ego – at your real situation. The biggest obstacles that stand between a company and its long-term success are the human elements. Things like personal ambition, fear, and even experience can cloud the vision of a company's leaders. Pressures to produce immediate results are compounded by the construction of compensation plans and the impatient expectations of the board of directors.

I've had the experience of seeing the president of a company ignore action plans that addressed changing conditions that had the potential to harm his company dramatically. Reminding him of the list of negative consequences that the market research said he could depend on if no action was taken, he replied (as if he were Alfred E. Newman himself), "Don't worry." With his head deep in the sand, he was betting against the probabilities because "staying the course" would have made fewer ripples with the board of directors. I wasn't around when he was shown the way out, but I know that his job wasn't the only one cut. He set a 20-something-year-old company that moved from a regional success, to a respected global entity, into an uncontrolled spiral that saw them later absorbed by their largest competitor. He led them into major lay-offs of lifelong employees, and repositioned the enterprise as a diminutive 30% of its former self within months.

Within the regular failures, poor planning processes, and less-than-thoughtful decisions described here, there are also examples of good marketing practices that work with unfailing certainty to keep a company alive and growing. That is, if all the conditions are in place for the success. Among those condition that must be in place is a culture that permits a formal planning structure. A company uses this process to reduce the influence of human factors, like ego, bias and experience, in order to force decisions based on real and verified information. If used correctly, the planning process will identify market changes and force the right questions to answer.

There is a certain hopelessness that permeates a business that is in decline. Yet, knowing the market, its current conditions, and seeing the problems clearly enough to be asking the right questions, helps divine the solutions that are available. Take a look at the recording industry that went from selling copyrighted vinyl records through the 1970's, to following the digital age by producing music on CD's in the 80's, but were unprepared when the internet produced the ultimate delivery system for consumers that included downloads and file sharing. Instead of looking forward and having a plan before consumers took control, they threw money at their legal departments and went to war with their consumers. Instead of asking, "How will people have access to our product and how can we prepare to serve them," their mindset was, "How can we stop them from stealing copyrighted material from us?" One company, from outside the music industry, looked at the problem for what it really was. With iTunes, Apple Computer revolutionized music delivery by accepting the new conditions of the market and providing a solution that fit.

Among the most reliable examples of how business should be done can be observed in the aisles of your local grocery store. The merchant itself isn't the example – they can come and go. Yet, stand in the toothpaste aisle. Look around where you buy laundry detergent and breakfast cereal. The packaging materials and designs may be moderately different, but the brands today are the same brands that dominated the shelves since the advent of the supermarket. Colgate-Palmolive, General Mills, and the others that continue to reign, do so because they systematically go to battle every day for inches of shelf space that return so much to the company's bottom line. They have systematic strategies for creating consumer buying habits, for retaining customers, for preempting their competitor's challenges, and for extending their brands to gain more shelf space.

Their marketing is comprehensive to the extent that they are structured in their recruiting, hiring, and mentoring the best talent from the best schools. Like a professional sports team, they know who will be able to play in their league and compete to get the most promising candidates. Like a sports team, they know that their schemes and systems cannot be understood and executed to the highest level of perfection by anyone coming off the street. Like a sports team, they practice the science of marketing with urgency and perfection, and recognize that it requires the ability to look downfield and adjust to changing conditions. They manage their markets from good intelligence at every level possible. What kind of detergent do you put in your dishwasher? What soap do you have in your hand when you wash? What do you spread on your bagel? Is it a brand you regularly buy? That's not an accident.

When you drop a product in your shopping cart, the company you chose knew that on a very personal level you were looking for some specific values and benefits. A peanut butter company blasts that their product has "no cholesterol." If that is something that troubles you, you may put it in your shopping cart without asking if the others on the shelf actually had cholesterol. Yes, they advertise their brands. They package with appealing characteristics that have been pre-proven in focus groups. They offer incentives to the retailer for beneficial shelf positioning. Yet, all of these investments actually support a customer need that existed. There's no guesswork in their execution. The product in your grocery cart is their reward for carefully planning. In the end, that results in stability for their company and security for their families.

ARE YOU PREPARED TO HEAR WHAT CONSUMERS TELL YOU?

The world changes with astounding speed. From obscurity, to the Presidency of the United States, one of the clearest examples of perfect marketing put Barack Obama in the White House. The strategy was born from understanding the wants and needs of the electorate, the weaknesses and strengths of the candidate, and the vulnerabilities and advantages of all viable foes. Through a range of the distractions and potential traps that one finds before them in a political campaign, they stayed focused, and away from sensation as much as possible. The opponent's campaign, in contrast, seemed to make several decisions that failed to reach the uncommitted voters.

Since Ronald Reagan and Newt Gingrich, the Republican Party in the United States has had a well-defined identity. There are very fundamental planks on their platform that appeal to many. Yet, in many respects, the electorate in 2008 took one of those planks and hit the Party's core squarely over the head. While political pundits and analysts will offer their opinions of why the election was won by Obama, the election was an excellent example to anyone involved in the marketing of any service or product. It provides a clear example of setting a specific goal, understanding the key elements that had to be in place in order to be successful, recognizing the dynamics of the world we live in, and being prepared to respond to any crisis within the framework of the long-term strategy.

On the other hand, not reading why the primary elections produced

John McCain as the candidate, the Republican Party completely missed the message coming from the market, and invested in selling what their popular membership wasn't buying anymore. Instead of following the electorate, the decision makers were acting on other facts and truths that were solidly supported by their testing, as testing is often done (with a bias to justify a conclusion that has already been made). Instead of asking what would appeal to the uncommitted electorate, they adopted tactics that appealed to the party as defined by a core of people that were too insignificant to sway the outcome.

By nominating John McCain, the general membership of the Republican Party rejected the type of candidates that professed the ideas and views that were closest to the core values of the party. By nominating a proven political "maverick," the voice of the party selected someone who was not the popular choice of the leaders at the platform's center. But instead of seeing the opportunity to reach a redefined party electorate, which took its shape in response to the current conditions of the country and the world, they seemed to make a series of strategic decisions to move the party back to its core identity. They took steps to assure the GOP's base that they could be comfortable with a McCain ticket.

First, they selected Sarah Palin as the running mate. She was a God-fearing, pro-life, anti-taxation, deregulating, conservative woman with state executive experience and popularity unmatched among Governors in the US. They moved aggressively, launching rhetoric and a campaign direction that pleased their delegates. The Republican Convention was electrified. Yet, her positioning may have ignored what their popular membership was telling them.

In the kind of market response that isn't unusual in any political campaign, business, or organization, there was little evidence that the energy within the party was focused on becoming more of what the people asked for. Instead, every action appeared to answer the question, "How can we save what we stand for?" The party didn't accept that the majority of those registered and voting in the primaries were sending the message that they liked what John McCain was saying that was different from what the others seeking the party nomination were saying. The polling booths during the primaries said the membership of the party wanted the guy who earned a reputation for separating himself from the "party line," reaching across the aisle, and getting stuff done. The popular Republican electorate voted that they didn't want Romney, Giuliani or others more in-tune with the GOP's standard platform. Yet, the party selected a VP candidate who spoke to the values of the party's core leadership.

She became a popular sensation. She energized the base and drew crowds that McCain could never draw on his own. The ticket preached a message of "change," but Palin's stump speeches contained many of the themes and a comfortable vigor that her party would not have gotten through McCain. The ticket spoke of change, yet Palin was tutored by former Bush staffers and was the voice of her party's status quo.

The Republicans in 2008 adopted a campaign that didn't crystallize what could be expected from the ticket should they ascend to the top offices in the land. Terrorism and homeland security issues, two wars, four dollars per gallon for gasoline, record budget deficits, record trade deficits, job losses, an actively aggressive Russia, a reneging North Korea, impossible health care, a failing education system, fears regarding global warming, increasing crime, and ultimately the collapse of the world's financial markets created a disenchanted American population. McCain was very strong with repeating white voters, which a few elections ago would have earned him the Presidency. First-time voters and the growing non-white population determined the result.

To the majority of the electorate, Obama's message was considered clearer, calmer, and more consistent than McCain's. The Democratic candidate avoided giving power to the stirring charges and controversies that were being raised on a regular basis. The opposition made efforts to cast doubt on his character, judgment, and patriotism.

They attempted to incite fear, when the market was looking for sound reasoning and solutions. The voter didn't care about a past minister or a former college activist when they were wondering how they would put gas in their car so they could go to interview for the job that they needed so badly. The people voting were down to the last egg in their refrigerator and the oil in their furnace was almost run dry.

That was the pre-election backdrop. Add that tax dollars were being committed to rescue a group of poorly run businesses in a country built on the premise that only the strong should survive. The general voting population wasn't accepting the negative character and inadequate experience messages as issues pertinent to any discussion about what this country really needed. With weeks to go, the impact of Sarah Palin actually pushed the Republican candidate ahead in the polling. Yet, the lead was given away by not knowing the needs, fears, and wants of the "uncommitted" voters in their market.

All of the Republican strategist's decisions were based on solid history and sound linear logic. Their actions helped to lock-in their member-ship, but did little to inspire the independent and uncommitted voter. After the election, polling of Republican Party members has confirmed that Sarah Palin was one of their party's most popular figures. But, appealing to GOP members was not enough to win the election.

Sympathetic pundits will say the economy's collapse caused the turn around. Yet, from Obama's side, it was a masterful exploitation of the marketing mix that hadn't been seen in politics for many years. This was textbook consumer marketing. The Obama campaign focused on positioning their party to address the concerns of the people. The Republican strategists positioned the concerns of the people within the context of their party. It matters little how popular a candidate might be with the party's most loyal members. The only thing that matters is who will get the most votes.

Tactically, the Democratic candidate chartered un-traveled territory. The Obama camp declined the government's matching financial support in favor of a fundraising strategy that could attract unlimited donations to a treasury that would have unprecedented power in delivering their message. Their "ground game" included thousands of individuals knocking on doors, working phone banks, organizing voter registrations, and tracking their progress. They created a voting base that had never been involved in political elections before. They focused on uncommitted and undecided voters. They keyed in on modern communication technology and the new generation that grew up being influenced by its power.

They delivered their product succinctly without any conflicting messages. They acted confidently, with a keen understanding of their vulnerabilities, and refused to engage in battles that could not be won. The Obama campaign was not without missteps. They never imploded from them, however. They exhibited calm resolve, stayed tight-lipped, and used their errors to help them become stronger. Through the good news and bad, they always showed the same face to the voter.

The Obama campaign was proof of the fact that there is no such thing as mass marketing. They had put together a grassroots organization unlike any ever seen. They set a record in contributions without any measurable revenues coming in from PACs, the Democratic Party, or personal contributions. The Republican Party's treasury was over 30% greater than the Democrat's. But where the dollars transferred to votes, Obama's individual campaign donors through the end of October 2008 added up to 91% of his nearly $640 million versus McCain's treasury total of $360 million. They used the tools of the day – capitalizing on YouTube and other internet sites to keep the message focused. They understood the mood of the American people, the current conditions of the market, and the key factors of success – and laid out a near perfect strategy, stayed on point, and made history. It was an historic occasion that saw the first African-American elected President of the United States. For businesses, however, it is an historic example of what happens when the strategies to do anything are based on an understanding of the conditions and opportunities of the day – and not on how things have always been done.

Regardless of your political leaning, this is a campaign whose fundamentals can be applied to adding revenue to your business. Through the Republican primaries, John McCain's campaign had many of the same characteristics as Obama's. He too was unlikely to prevail against the expected leaders. His message suited a disgruntled voter base. In the early stages of the campaign, Giuliani and Clinton seemed to be the names that would appear on the 2008 ballot. Yet, McCain and Obama better understood the pulse of the people. Again, successful marketing of anything depends on meeting the needs and wants of the customer. The products that prevail are the ones that provide a value that meets the consumer's expectation and that are positioned in an appealing way. In Obama's case, seeing how far the virtually unknown candidate had come defines the most important lesson for marketers.

You must start with a specific goal that makes sense for you in your environment. You must be honest about where your opportunities really exist within the current market conditions. The factors that are critical for your success must be defined and in place. The actions you take must always move you closer to your success. With a profound understanding of the market and a focus on the consumer's needs and wants, success is limitless. Who you are today matters little if you know who you want to be tomorrow, and you take a strategic approach.

PONDERING THE CRAFT

I once was in a discussion with a sales executive about the things we needed to do to be more successful in the marketplace. He spoke about what had worked in the past that should be repeated. He kept saying that he's been in the business for twenty years and that he "knows the market." The fact was, however, that he and his sales organization hadn't been reeling in any new business, and as he kept repeating the word "market," it occurred to me that he was referring to a place that, in his mind, was static and fixed. His view of the "market" was a noun, like a piece of furniture. Furniture is something that can become more comfortable the longer you sit in it. No one is thinking about absolute vulnerability as they recline in their favorite lounge chair.

I suggest that it's important to think of the word "market" as a verb. It is defined by the actions that are taken to satisfy the needs of consumers in the marketplace. When "market" is used as a noun, it should be in the same sense that "heartbeat" is a noun. To market is to keep an enterprise alive.

To market successfully is a process of constantly learning and adjusting to address a dynamic set of conditions. Being in a business for twenty years has no benefit if you aren't continuing to adapt to it. The old expression about the sales profession, "that you are only as good as your last order," has an absolute application to the profession of marketing, too. The competitive sales plan comes from knowing the marketplace and offering a value-proposition that answers its needs. For the sales personnel to be successful, they need to depend on the intelligence and support that comes from their company's strategic market planning.

To be successful in marketing, one needs to understand the psychology, the culture, and the geography of the intended consumer. Success comes from anticipating and adapting to technological advances, demographic shifts, and economic realities of the market. Smart marketing knows that change is the only constant to depend upon.

You may assume that having young and energetic people to help create the perfect marketing mix to address a demographic of young people is a requirement. You may seek people with a long history of racing automobiles to help sell high-performance auto parts. It is normal to think that the best way to understand a guitar player is to be a guitar player. But, that kind of assumption is a bit like saying that the best veterinarians would be horses. More to the point, it's like saying that selling cars to Americans requires an American-drafted strategy. It's like saying that the right person to transform IBM should have been nurtured through its culture. Against the evidence, that's all plain wrong.

To market any of these products to their maximum potential, you need someone who knows how to research and interpret information. They need to develop an impartial and unbiased approach to learning, filtering, and processing the factors that will influence their success. They need to be intelligent. They need to understand the "industry neutral" processes of strategic market planning. Once that is established, you need someone with wisdom and courage to lead the changes that the information dictates.

The structure of the company, its organization, and the direction of its plan must be determined by the conditions of the market and the company's internal resources. Often businesses of the last century have been sales-driven, with marketing resources used more as a way of supporting a faulty sales plan, and not as a way to secure a long-term future. Consider the leading brands of the 1950's. How are they positioned and who are they today? Technologies emerge, the culture evolves, and the consumer's needs change.   The stable brands developed by the General Mills and Proctor and Gambles of the world have always been managed by the strongest principles of consumer marketing and product management that every company can adapt. It's a process that sets the stage for long-term strategic thinking, innovating, and the defending of marketshare in a dynamic environment. The strategic planning at tobacco-born Philip Morris led to acquiring a non-tobacco company part of its survival plan.   The tobacco company became Altria and distanced itself from its growingly taboo heritage.   That too, was part of a plan.   Improved security for the company, the shareholders, and the employees, required adapting to societal evolution.   Marketing requires keeping one's eyes open for opportunities and threats within the changes that come at a remarkable speed.

Consider the swift and head-spinning changes of the last half-century. Americans born during the Baby Boom saw television become the new forum for mass communication.   They witnessed Kennedy's mastery of its power to defeat Nixon, and were the first to say, "I want that" as the stream of Christmas-time toy ads stirred young imaginations between Popeye and Rocky the Flying Squirrel.   They saw the deaths of a President, an assassin, a Civil Rights activist, and a Presidential contender on TV.   They saw a man step onto the surface of the moon. They watched the Vietnam War during dinner-time news broadcasts bringing daily body counts and advancement reports.   Soap Operas got their name specifically because of their marketing strength in establishing brand-named household products with housewives in the 1960's.

Television emerged as the medium to deliver mass-positioning of the political message.   Social barriers were trampled in the 1960's. Television broadcast irreverent satire with programs like Laugh-in and the Smothers Brothers.   The war protestors on campuses across the US, and the riots at the Chicago Democratic Convention were broadcast on TV.   There were race riots, and National Guardsmen were posted on the corners from Oakland to DC to keep peace among the burned-out building shells. The marketplace became a segmented array of tastes and opinions. Information was instantaneous and everything that the country believed was challenged. There wasn't a single direction the nation's collective ethical and moral compass pointed. With so many voices, so many positions, so distinctly separate ideals and personalities, how could you sell them?

Today, the world is even more different. America has been attacked on its own soil. Air travel is cumbersome and frightening. News is delivered through several dozen cable TV channels with reports as divisive as anytime in history. Internet bloggers have become a formidable power in the political process. There are no more paperboys leaving the news under the welcome mat at the front porch.

Materials evolved from steel to carbon fiber. The power of the Univac from the 1960's can be found in the average 5th grader's back pack. How things are invented and where things are made are constantly changing. Stewardship of the world's environment demands a more enlightened attention to how the things we do and make impact the earth, influencing what and how people consume. To stay afloat, every company needs to be alert to opportunities these changes provide and recognize that accepted paradigms may not last more than the blink of an eye.

Today, the white majority is shrinking and America is quickly becoming a dual language society. A culture that was spawned in the most depressed sections of Compton and New York has become integrated into the privileged white prep school culture throughout the country. The generation characterized on television during the 1960's as student protestors and antiestablishment activists are revealed forty years later as well-invested retirees living in villas on the Coast. The oppressive and stereotypical attitudes about women and African-Americans, to which organizations like NOW and the NAACP were originally devoted, have changed. And the beat goes on.

Ask the sales manager who knows his (or her) market what he (or she) did fifteen years ago that is going to help him grow the business now. What is known about the market as the aging Baby Boomer generation (that did not replace themselves as the previous generations had) dies off? With an all-time record 300,000,000 Americans, how will the proven methods of the past help to sustain an enterprise as Hispanic, Asian, and Indian cultures drive the population numbers higher against a shrinking white population?

Marketing is restless, which is good news or bad news depending upon the structure of your enterprise and its flexibility to adapt. There is no final success. Marketing is about possibilities and real potential achieved in a dynamic environment. Strategic market planning is necessary because no company is ever safe. There is one thing a company can be sure of. You can know with certainty that some company somewhere is plotting to take the marketshare you own and the position you have earned. Expect that their planning process will be as thoughtful, complete and measured as yours. Every company is vulnerable. The strongest do fall. Success can be gained and sustained only by putting relevant plans into action.

In addition to using strategic planning to keep your rudder trim in a changing environment, the plan can also deal with the human characteristics of those within your company that need monitoring. A recent list of the "25 greatest businesses to close" suggests every company should have tools to make its leaders accountable. It should also help them to stay ethical. Ten of the twenty-five companies listed were felled by fraud, corruption, scandal, and the abuse of trust. From Adelphi to Zzzz Best, the methods of deception and mismanagement are born from basic human greed and the intoxication of power. Enron and WorldCom's "C-Level" managers destroyed lives and cost innocent investors their nest eggs. Eighty-five thousand jobs were lost at Arthur Anderson when the public lost trust in the established "Big 8" accounting firm due to the illegal accounting tricks perpetuated on behalf of Enron. Less public is the small business executive or middle-level manager who cheats his company through expensed lunches, trips, and gifts to his or her friends, family or paramours. If the saying, "A fish begins to stink from the top," has any truth, shouldn't there always be a way built into a company's planning to keep those at the top in check?

Marketing rarely is about the past unless it is to learn lessons from it that allow the enterprise to move forward.   One can learn from the past, but they should never market in it.   Learned lessons for one time period are not always applicable or even relevant in another.   Too often companies find themselves at risk because those who have grown success under a specific set of conditions are unwilling to adapt to new conditions.   Marketing is about anticipating.   Successful marketing comes from knowing your consumers, the trends in distribution, your competitor's capabilities, and their culture as well as you possibly can. It's about seeing trends and taking educated steps in a direction that prepares you to flourish.

Every day brings a new opportunity.   An invincible company doesn't exist.   Big doesn't mean smart.   TWA and Pan Am once dominated international flights and today they have no meaningful presence. These were giant brands once thought to be invincible in their markets.

Changes in market conditions create the chance for the most alert to rediscover themselves.   Sometimes it's the simplest of ideas that make the greatest impact.   The era of the "housewife" ended and the emergence of the full-service bakery in the supermarket brought a threat to the sales of baking soda.   Arm and Hammer responded by selling us their product to make our refrigerators smell better.

Don't confuse marketing with advertising.   Advertising is only one element of a complete marketing mix.   It's the most public element, the one that grabs the consumer's attention and captures the imagination.   But advertising that is not supported by the strategic management of the other elements of the marketing mix is plain stupid.

An advertising agency likes to win awards.   They feel successful if their ads become part of the popular culture.   They get paid for what they sell to their clients, regardless of whether what they sell works. Although humorous and temporarily woven into the fabric of the popular culture of the time, "Joe Isuzu" car company ads and the "Where's the Beef" Wendy's fast food ads did nothing to grow sales. They failed to create a position for the product in the consumer's mind that encouraged any sales. They did nothing to change a buying habit by addressing a consumer need or want. Neither articulated a core value of the products they were pitching. Joe was a liar. The little old lady was shrill. The ads were a pop sensation. The ads were useless.

A few sensational ads do work. Among the most famous advertising successes in history was a famed Apple spot that aired during the 1984 Super Bowl. It positioned its new Macintosh line against IBM by crashing a sledgehammer against an Orwellian "Big Brother" image in a well-produced, futuristic sixty-second film. "On January 24th, Apple Computer will introduce Macintosh. And you'll see why 1984 won't be like '1984," the voice over said. The single ad, run before the largest annual television audience in the US, saved the struggling company. Expensive, powerful, and highly memorable to anyone who saw it, the Macintosh ad is considered by many to be among the most important broadcast ads ever.

In the 1984 market, there were few other recognizable names in meaningful personal computing other than IBM and Apple. The Commodore 64 sold a ton of product, but it was a glorified toy that only served the market by exposing the possibilities of home computing to the masses. The world was based on IBM. IBM and the range of derived DOS-based computers were the "serious" products. Computers were becoming a growing necessity but were hard to learn to use without help. Pricing of products made them more accessible, but there was still resistance by all but the most technically savvy because of the challenging learning curve. The DOS system was less than intuitive and programs like Lotus and WordPerfect were just beginning to make headway. In the Super Bowl ad, Apple overtly challenged IBM in front of an entire nation. They boldly hit the giant squarely where they were most vulnerable in the most visible and public forum possible. There was only one way that it couldn't be considered foolish.

For any advertising to succeed, the rest of the marketing mix must be in place. In this case, the product had to be better, and not just marginally. The Macintosh had to significantly address the needs and wants of a growing consumer base in a way that redefined the consumer's expectation for personal computing. The product had to be reliable with a short learning curve and friendly ergonomics. The distribution had to be in place with stocked shelves and knowledgeable customer support. The price had to add value over the competitor. It had to reduce work and increase productivity. It had to literally neutralize every advantage IBM held in personal computing. It had to take entire segments of the market away from Big Brother and it did. On all counts, they were ready.

Macintosh redefined entire industries. Engineering, graphic design, music, and video production, all found more potential for making money and saving time with the Macintosh. The Mac made these industries more accessible to more people. Apple's key to success was to understand how people did their jobs, and to provide a tool to do them better without extensive training. They redefined the human interface with the machine that ultimately set the standards that Windows would later follow. Using a Mac was not tedious, confusing, time consuming, or dependent upon the user understanding a complex operating system. Compared to the PC world, the products were fast, reliable, and greatly expandable. There was a range of software support for every meaningful job. They were actually fun. While the button-down collar segment largely held on to IBM-inspired PC models, Apple found new markets.

Effective marketing is understanding change as an opportunity for growth. The stability of any company is only ensured through a long-term and short-term strategy that monitors current conditions, anticipates future trends, and identifies threats. Strong marketing is a process of vigilance, confidence, and courage that welcomes change and guides a company successfully through it. It's a process that evaluates strengths and weaknesses, and reconstructs them, to give the company its best competitive advantage. A strong plan focuses effort for the best measurable result, while neutralizing vulnerabilities. An effective marketing plan looks both outward and inward, bringing viable tactics that work in concert for the long and short-term. Marketing is never arrogant. It is never inflexible. It never assumes to "know it all." It respects change. It always is based on strong information and a sound plan that fits the times. It is useful everywhere business is expected to grow.

The most certain fact that any company needs to keep as the background of its planning is that the odds are against them. If your short-term plan isn't in accord with a measured and strategically thoughtful plan for long-term survival, or if you have no idea where you hope to be in the upcoming years, it is most certain that you are on your way out.

Businesses must act as if they are absolutely vulnerable – because regardless of how comfortable they may feel, how loyal their customers are, how established they may be in the marketplace, and the distance they have placed between their competitors - they are always vulnerable to failure. A well run company that enjoys sustained prosperity is often the company that sets aside the time to look at itself objectively, and sets a determined course for its future. You can set out to do something and achieve it 5% of the time or you can adopt a culture of strategic planning and meet your objectives over 80% of the time. I know what most companies will do. But, I also know what smart people can do. A company can be whatever it wants to be if it understands, and plans for the realistic opportunities in the marketplace.

Index

BRAINWORKS BOOKS
Philadelphia, Pennsylvania
www.tamalm.com

www.ingramcontent.com/pod-product-compliance
Lightning Source LLC
Chambersburg PA
CBHW031932190326
41519CB00007B/506